3

Arthur Miller's

DEATH
OF A
SALESMAN

A CONTEMPORARY
LITERARY VIEWS BOOK

Edited and with an Introduction by
HAROLD BLOOM

3 5 7 9 8 6 4 2

ISBN: 0-7910-3681-2 (hc)
       0-7910-4118-2 (pb)

Chelsea House Publishers
1974 Sproul Road, Suite 400
P.O. Box 914
Broomall, PA 19008-0914

Contents

User's Guide

This volume is designed to present biographical, critical, and bibliographical information on Arthur Miller and *Death of a Salesman*. Following Harold Bloom's introduction, there appears a detailed biography of the author, discussing the major events in his life and his important literary works. Then follows a thematic and structural analysis of the work, in which significant themes, patterns, and motifs are traced. An annotated list of characters supplies brief information on the chief characters in the work.

A selection of critical extracts, derived from previously published material by leading critics, then follows. The extracts consist of statements by the author on his work, early reviews of the work, and later evaluations down to the present day. The items are arranged chronologically by date of first publication. A bibliography of Miller's writings (including a complete listing of all the books he has written, cowritten, edited, and translated), a list of additional books and articles on him and on *Death of a Salesman,* and an index of themes conclude the volume.

Harold Bloom is Sterling Professor of the Humanities at Yale University and Henry W. and Albert A. Berg Professor of English at the New York University Graduate School. He is the author of twenty books and the editor of more than thirty anthologies of literature and literary criticism.

Professor Bloom's works include *Shelley's Mythmaking* (1959), *The Visionary Company* (1961), *Blake's Apocalypse* (1963), *Yeats* (1970), *A Map of Misreading* (1975), *Kabbalah and Criticism* (1975), and *Agon: Towards a Theory of Revisionism* (1982). *The Anxiety of Influence* (1973) sets forth Professor Bloom's provocative theory of the literary relationships between the great writers and their predecessors. His most recent books are *The American Religion* (1992) and *The Western Canon* (1994).

Professor Bloom earned his Ph.D. from Yale University in 1955 and has served on the Yale faculty since then. He is a 1985 MacArthur Foundation Award recipient and served as the Charles Eliot Norton Professor of Poetry at Harvard University in 1987–88. He is currently the editor of the Chelsea House series Major Literary Characters and Modern Critical Views, and other Chelsea House series in literary criticism.

Introduction

HAROLD BLOOM

The dramatic critic Eric Bentley defines the central flaw in *Death of a Salesman* as Arthur Miller's inability (and consequently ours) to know whether the play's obsessive concern is politics or sex. Bentley's point is accurate, and the assertions of some feminist critics that Willy Loman's tragedy centers on "the politics of sex" seem to me unpersuasive. As a playwright, Arthur Miller works always in the shadow of Henrik Ibsen, a dangerous influence for Miller because Ibsen essentially was a daemonic dramatist, trollish and Shakespearean, always closer to a cosmos of elemental forces, like those in *King Lear* and *Macbeth*, than to the social world of politics and economics. Even Ibsen's social dramas conceal trollish energies behind their societal masks; Hedda Gabler is more a troll than a victim of the patriarchy, and can be regarded as Iago's sister. But Miller always has imitated what he interprets as a social reformer in Ibsen, forgetting James Joyce's wry observation that Ibsen was no more a feminist than Joyce was a bishop. Social forces certainly affect Hedda Gabler, but Ibsen does not represent them as controlling her life or as determining her fate. Miller, in contrast, wants to give us a Willy Loman who is destroyed by social energies. Fortunately for the continued dramatic validity of *Death of a Salesman,* something deeper than Miller's political polemic pervades the play and makes it more than a parody of "the American Dream" of upward mobility, so that Willy Loman finally escapes the dubious fate of being a poor man's Jay Gatsby.

For a dramatic protagonist to impress us as legitimately "tragic," she or he must possess aesthetic dignity, which is not necessarily identical with human dignity. All bad tragedies, as Oscar Wilde might have said, are sincere, and Arthur Miller's sincerity is palpable. Miller has written some bad tragedies, but *Death of a Salesman* certainly is not one of them. With all its faults and ambiguities, it rivals Eugene O'Neill's *Long Day's Journey into Night* as a modern American tragic drama, even though, like O'Neill's work, it seems to me of a lesser eminence than the best tragicomedies of Tennessee Williams. Like O'Neill, Miller essentially is the tragedian of what Sigmund Freud called "Family Romances." *Death of a Salesman* is more the tragedy of a family than it is of an individual or of a society. Doubtless I am influenced by the experience of once having attended a performance of the play in Yiddish translation, which I found to be both illuminating and harrowing, though highly ironic, since Miller labors in his drama to render Willy as the American Everyman and the Lomans as an archetypal American family. Perhaps Miller succeeds in this effort, though at a certain cost, by blending Willy and the Lomans into a common grayness, so that they lack all color or exuberance and yield much of their pathos to a vision of social reductiveness, as if they were victims purely of the false dreams of their nation. What *Death of a Salesman* most lacks is a Shakespearean or Ibsenite *foregrounding:* a sense of the involvement of tradition both in Willy's loneliness and in his family's inability to understand his yearning quality, his dream of an excessive familial love that might assuage his loneliness.

Even though Willy Loman's aesthetic dignity depends more upon pathos than upon a nonexistent tragic grandeur, his dignity seems to me real enough to have sustained the play and to go on sustaining it as we approach the Millennium. Miller's social ironies mostly weaken the drama, yet the ironies of familial love in *Death of a Salesman* constitute its ongoing strength. Though it is forty-four years since I saw the play in its Yiddish version, I remain seared by the peculiar power of that performance, which accentuated the anguish of the Lomans' family romance and the dignity of Willy's desperate failure to be what he yearned to be, a good father and a good husband. If Willy has tragic stature, it is because he is exiled from himself, and so can win no victory whatsoever. We are terribly moved by Willy's confused conviction that, if he is not successful, then he will not deserve to be loved by his family. No possible success could assuage Willy's tormented yearning to be popular, to be loved. It is a peculiar tragedy that Willy is destroyed by love, and by the inevitable ambivalences that attend family romances. The American dream in Jay Gatsby is a High Romantic vision of Eros, grotesquely represented by his nostalgia for the banal Daisy, and yet still an authentic vision, because Gatsby himself, as mediated by the narrator Nick Carraway, is anything but banal. Willy Loman's American dream is rescued from aesthetic banality precisely because it is possessed by the enigmas that mark a guilty dream. Poor Willy, who desired so intensely only to be a good husband and a good father, destroys himself because of the guilty realization that pragmatically he has become both a bad husband and a bad father. I do not think that Willy Loman has the authentic dignity of a tragic protagonist, but his sincere pathos does have authentic aesthetic dignity, because he does not die the death of a salesman. He dies the death of a father, perhaps not the universal father, but a father central enough to touch the anguish of the universal. ❖

Biography of Arthur Miller

Arthur Miller was born on October 17, 1915, to Isadore and Augusta Barnett Miller, a well-to-do Jewish couple. The first fourteen years of his life were spent in upscale Harlem; then, when the stock market crash of 1929 and the subsequent depression nearly ruined his father, a manufacturer of ladies' coats, Miller's family moved to Brooklyn. He was an indifferent student, and upon graduating from Abraham Lincoln High School in 1932 he found that his grades were not good enough to get him into college—which, in any event, his family could not afford. Miller took a series of odd jobs, then worked for a year as a shipping clerk in an automobile parts warehouse. During this time he first began to read literature extensively. In 1934 Miller was accepted at the University of Michigan, where he enrolled as a journalism student and began to write plays.

His first two dramas, *No Villain* (1936) and *Honors at Dawn* (1937), both won minor awards, which encouraged him to pursue his ambitions as a playwright. By the time he graduated in 1938 he had completed one more play, as well as discovering the works of Henrik Ibsen; these became a lasting influence on his own writing. In 1939 he wrote a play, *The Golden Years,* for the Federal Theatre Project. This was followed by four or five other plays, none of which were produced at the time and all of which he found unsatisfactory. It was not until 1944 that he wrote *The Man Who Had All the Luck,* the first notable play of his mature period, and a qualified success in its author's eyes as well. It won the Theatre Guild National Award. This was followed by a nonfiction book, *Situation Normal* (1944), based on interviews with American servicemen, and by *Focus* (1945), a novel about anti-Semitism.

Miller began to receive increasing critical notice with the production of his play *All My Sons* (1947), an Ibsenesque drama centered on the revelation of a small manufacturer's having supplied defective equipment under a government contract during the war. It was the next play that secured his reputation: *Death of a Salesman* (1949), the story of a failed traveling salesman and his two sons, became an instant classic of the American theatre and was awarded a Pulitzer Prize.

After publishing an adaptation of Henrik Ibsen's *An Enemy of the People* (1951), Miller wrote *The Crucible* (1953), which dealt with the Salem witch trials of 1692. This play was also well received, but it attracted critical attention of another sort. Miller's history of affiliation with leftist organizations brought him under the eye of Senator Joseph McCarthy and the House Un-American Activities Committee (HUAC) during their investigations of alleged Communist infiltration of American institutions. Miller freely testified before the committee in his own behalf, but refused its requests that he name others who had been similarly involved. In the political climate of the time *The Crucible* was, perhaps understandably, read as a commentary on the McCarthyites' activities. Though HUAC found him an insufficiently friendly witness, Miller's career survived the experience, and his *A View from the Bridge,* presented in 1955 on a double bill with his short play *A Memory of Two Mondays,* brought him a second Pulitzer Prize.

In 1956 Miller divorced his wife of many years, Mary Grace Slattery Miller—whom he had married in 1940 and who had supported him and their two children during his unremunerative early writing career—and married the actress Marilyn Monroe. (His screenplay for the 1961 film *The Misfits,* directed by John Huston and starring Monroe and Clark Gable, was originally conceived as a vehicle for her.) After five years the second marriage ended in divorce, and in 1962 Miller married photographer Inge Morath, with whom he had two children; he also collaborated with her on several books, writing text to accompany her pictures.

In 1963 Miller published *Jane's Blanket,* a children's book. The next year his *After the Fall,* a semi-autobiographical, almost novelistic play whose action spans several decades, was produced to mixed notices; some critics panned it as self-indulgent, while others have praised its complex exploration of character and moral issues. It was followed by *Incident at Vichy* (1965), a short play about Nazism and anti-Semitism in Vichy France, and by *The Price* (1968) and *The American Clock* (produced 1980; published 1982), both of which return to Miller's earlier themes of domestic life and family conflicts. Other recent Miller plays include *The Archbishop's Ceiling* (produced 1977; published 1984), *The Last Yankee* (1991), *Broken Glass* (1994), and several short plays.

Besides his plays, Miller's other works include *I Don't Need You Anymore* (1967), a collection of short stories (an expanded edition was published in 1987 as *The Misfits and Other Stories*); *In Russia* (1969) and *In the Country* (1977), both with Inge Morath; and *The Theater Essays of Arthur Miller* (1978), a volume of his previously uncollected short essays and criticism. Miller's trip to Beijing in 1983 to direct *Death of a Salesman* was written up in an autobiographical volume, *Salesman in Beijing* (1984), while *Timebends: A Life* (1987) is a more formal autobiography. Miller continues to live and write in Connecticut. ✣

Thematic and Structural Analysis

A great scholar of the western literary tradition has defined realism as the "serious" representation of the ordinary and of the life of the lower classes. Few works of American literature are so deliberately "realist" in this sense as Arthur Miller's *Death of a Salesman*. The play dramatizes the late-life madness and suicide of Willy Loman, an undistinguished traveling salesman who lives in a small house in Brooklyn with his wife. His very name is meant to emphasize his "low" position in society. And his despair is the result of an accumulation of the most ordinary of grievances. He and his beloved older son have deeply disappointed one another. He has betrayed his wife's unwavering faith in him. He is losing the ability to perform his job and thus to provide for himself and his wife and to assist his two grown children. And the departure of his grown children has left him terribly lonely. He decides that the best way for him to help the family he believes he has failed is to commit suicide so that they may collect money on his life insurance policy. The play documents his manic, distracted, and bitterly sad final two days.

The structure of the play is designed to reflect Willy's volatile state of mind. Rather than the conventional pattern of several acts, each with a number of short scenes, *Death of a Salesman* contains only two acts with no separate scenes. The action within the acts is broken up only according to the fluid and unpredictable wandering of Willy's thoughts. We move seamlessly between the present and the past as Willy recollects happier times with his boys or guilty moments with his mistress. We also move rapidly from exalted to despondent moods as Willy retreats into fantastic hopes or confronts the full difficulty of his situation. Small details—such as the sight of his wife mending stockings—can send Willy suddenly into an entirely different temporal frame of reference. The other characters are mystified by these sudden leaps, but the audience is enabled to see how Willy's troubled mind is working. "The way of telling the tale," as Arthur Miller himself put it, "in this sense, is as mad as Willy and as abrupt and suddenly lyrical. . . . There are no flashbacks in this play but only a mobile concurrency of past and present. . . . [My idea was] to cling to the process of Willy's mind as the form the story would take."

At the start of **Act 1**, Willy arrives home, carrying two suitcases with an exhausted and frazzled air. In response to the worried queries of Linda, his wife, he explains that he has "come back" instead of finishing his sales trip because he nearly had an accident while driving through Yonkers. He was so shaken by the incident that he turned around and drove home at ten miles per hour—which took him four hours. "I'm tired to the death," he says portentously to his wife as he sits beside her on the bed, "I couldn't make it, I just couldn't make it, Linda. . . . I suddenly couldn't drive any more. The car kept going off onto the shoulder, y'know?" Linda offers a number of possible explanations—the steering, his glasses—but Willy knows that the problem is his own distracted state. "Suddenly I realize that I'm goin' sixty miles an hour and I don't remember the last five minutes. I'm—I can't seem to—keep my mind to it." We learn that this is not the only time Willy has had such problems recently. Linda tries to get him to accept the fact that he needs to take time off "to relax his mind." She reminds him that he is sixty years old and urges him to request of his boss that he no longer be required to travel. After a spasm of prideful resistance to the idea of asking anything of the ungrateful son of the man for whom he originally went to work, Willy acquiesces and promises to talk to him in the morning.

Talk then turns to the subject of the children. We learn that the older of their two sons, Biff, has come from out West to visit, and that he and the younger son, Happy, went out "on a date" earlier in the evening. Linda takes great pleasure in seeing her boys together in the house again; but their presence only heightens Willy's sense of abandonment. "Figure it out," he says wryly. "Work a lifetime to pay off a house. You finally own it, and there's nobody to live in it." Linda responds with the kind of patient, self-sacrificing wisdom that characterizes her throughout the play: "Well, dear, life is a casting off. It's always that way." Willy is not placated. He can't understand why Biff has not made more of himself by age thirty-four. He is impatient with Linda's view that Biff still needs time to "find himself." "In the greatest country in the world," he says incredulously, "a young man with such—personal attractiveness—gets lost?" He claims several times that Biff is simply lazy. But his old proud affection for his son soon overcomes him and he directly contradicts himself. "There's one thing about Biff—he's not lazy," he says, completely forgetting his condemnation of a moment before. He tells Linda to go to sleep, as he promises to have a "nice talk" with Biff in the morning. He goes downstairs for a snack, drifting into happy reminiscences of Biff's popularity in high school and of how hard Biff used to work simonizing his father's red Chevy.

The boys, asleep in their childhood bedroom, are awakened by the unexpected sound of their father's voice. They arise, smoke, and converse as the sound of his talking to himself percolates at intervals into their range of hearing. In a stage note both brothers are described as tall, well-built, and sexually attractive. They are also both described as "lost." We are told that Biff, the older by two years, is more aware of being lost and is therefore more "worn" and less self-confident. We find out a great deal more about their respective situations and temperaments as they talk.

Happy enjoys the appearance of success. He has a merchandising job where he makes good money. He has an apartment of his own and plenty of women. He once believed that this was all he needed, but he finds that he is still frustrated and lonely. He confesses to Biff that he takes pleasure in seducing the wives or fiancées of executives in his company, and that he is not above taking a bribe now and again from a manufacturer who wants a contract. He is aware that these are "crummy characteristics," but he cannot help himself. He is contemptuous of the people he works with, and he longs to free himself from the pettiness of the business world—to "take off [his] shirt" and work with his "muscles" out-of-doors. But he cannot take up Biff's offer to come and work out West because he feels compelled to outdo the people around him, to prove his superiority to them, and to succeed on their terms. Although he knows it is shallow, he wants to feel the thrill of wearing expensive suits and having "the waves part" when he walks through the door. One senses that Happy has inherited his father's sense of inferiority and is driven to compensate for it. He is nonetheless genuinely concerned about his father, and in a bluff way he appeals to Biff to try to help. He tells Biff that most of their father's distracted talk seems to be addressed to him, that Willy is worried about how unsettled Biff seems to be, and that it might be best if Biff returned to New York. Perhaps, Happy suggests, they could go into business together.

Biff is in many ways like Happy, but, as Miller puts it in a stage note, "he has succeeded less, and his dreams are stronger and less acceptable." Biff tells Happy of his unhappiness in the years following high school, when he tried to work his way up in business. He could not see the point of riding the subway and plodding away fifty weeks a year in anticipation of two weeks of freedom. He found "grubbing for money" demeaning, so he followed up on the urge to work outdoors and went out West. But he confesses that he has also been dissatisfied there. He loves the beauty of the landscape and the contact with nature, but the "twenty or thirty jobs" he has had do not seem to have amounted to much. He starts to think about whether or not he is building a future for himself, and he gets frightened and comes home. His plan this time is to approach Bill Oliver—the owner of a sporting goods store where he worked as a kid—and to ask him for a loan so that he might invest in a ranch. He is worried that Bill Oliver might remember that he stole a carton of basketballs from the store while he was employed there, but Happy assures him the incident has probably been forgotten. Genuine goodwill and affection between the brothers is conveyed as Happy immediately forgets his own worries in his excitement over Biff's new plan.

Their excitement is quickly checked, however, by the rising volume of their father's solitary voice. They silently listen as Willy maintains an imaginary conversation with Biff as a popular high school senior of sixteen years ago. Biff becomes disgusted and angered by the sorry spectacle Willy is making in front of his mother. Happy reiterates his appeal to Biff to come home and live nearby. "Isn't that terrible?" Happy says. "You gotta stick around. I don't know what to do about him. It's getting embarrassing." Biff responds only by turning out the light and cursing his father as the boys attempt to fall asleep.

The focus then shifts to Willy, lost in the midst of a sustained reminiscence of the rapport he once enjoyed with his boys, especially Biff. A great sense of warmth and mutual admiration is evoked as Willy recalls advising them about women, supervising them on small projects around the house, surprising them with a new punching bag, and promising to take Biff along on one of his business trips. We also detect the seed of later difficulties as Willy tries to impress his boys by exaggerating the importance and prestige of his job. He also tolerates Biff's propensity for petty thefts—in this case a football taken from the team locker room. And Willy shares Biff's contempt for a studious boy next door, Bernard, who tries to help Biff prepare for his exams. It is better, Willy tells his sons, to be athletic and well liked as they are, than to be bookish, "anemic," and unpopular like their diligent neighbor. Biff has been promised football scholarships by three schools, and Willy refuses to believe Bernard when he warns him that if Biff fails the state math exam he will lose these awards. We begin to see that Biff's and Happy's later restlessness and exaggerated self-estimation were fostered in them by their father in their childhood. Willy has a need to believe that his children are above the ordinary rules that have so cramped his own life, and he passes this belief on to Biff and Happy.

The deep insecurities beneath Willy's bluster are further revealed as his mind leaps to a different set of memories. Now we see him confessing to his wife that he had exaggerated his initial account of how much money he made on a recent sales trip. The truth is that he has barely made enough to pay the bills for the washing machine, dishwasher, vacuum cleaner, and other basic home appliances. "People don't take to me," he admits pathetically. "I talk too much . . . I don't have the right demeanor . . . I tell too many jokes . . . I'm fat, and foolish to look at . . . ." He remembers "cracking in the face" someone who called him "a walrus." His wife lovingly reassures him, but this causes his mind to jump guiltily to recollections of the flirtatious laughter of his mistress, who told him she picked him out from the other salesmen because of his sense of humor. He recalls buying her stockings, but this brings him abruptly back to the present again as he sees that his wife is sewing stockings as she sits with him. Ashamed by the implication that he deprives his wife of what he gives to his mistress, he angrily insists that Linda throw them out. "I won't have you mending stockings in this house!" he shouts. She patiently puts them in her pocket.

Willy's memories now come to a kind of harassing crescendo. The pleasantly nostalgic memories of Biff's high school athletic prowess now turn dark. Willy recalls being told that the young Biff is "too rough with the girls." He remembers his wife insisting that Biff return the stolen football. He remembers finding out that Biff was driving without a license. Worst of all, he remembers realizing that Biff was in real danger of failing math and losing his scholarship because his teacher believed he was arrogant and refused to give him a break, and his neighbor, Bernard, would not help him cheat on the state exam. It is significant of his own moral shortcomings that Willy insists that Bernard should help Biff cheat, and that he promises pompously to "have a talk" with the recalcitrant teacher. With characteristic blindness, however, Willy cannot see that by indulging Biff he has helped to create some of his dangerous character flaws. Alone in his kitchen in the middle of the night sixteen years later, Willy still fails to understand himself or his son as he screams at the walls: "Why is he stealing? What did I tell him? I never in my life told him anything but decent things." Happy comes down to the kitchen to try to quiet him, teasing him that he is "going to retire him for life." But Willy will not be reigned in. His voice continues to rise as he makes a desperate plea to the children who he believes have abandoned him: "Christ's sake, I couldn't get past Yonkers today! Where are you guys, where are you? The woods are burning! I can't drive a car!"

It is now the next-door neighbor's turn to try to calm Willy. Charley appears at the doorway in his pajamas, asking "Is everything all right?" Charley is a voice of resigned, almost cynical sanity in the play. In contrast to Willy, he is low-key, steady, and dispassionate. It is his studious son, Bernard, whom Biff and Willy mocked as a boy, but who is now a successful attorney, arguing cases in front of the Supreme Court. Charley's fundamental decency soon becomes apparent as he sends Happy to bed, sits down with Willy, endures some of his petty needling, and tries, as sensitively as possible, to help him. He suggests playing cards to help tire Willy out, and as they play he offers him a job. Willy immediately becomes insulted, however, and rejects the offer. Charley compliments Willy on the new ceiling he has installed in his house, and then gently tries again, advising Willy that he cannot go on for long in his present state. But Willy again gets testy, insisting that he has a perfectly good job. Charley gives up as Willy abruptly changes the topic to his son, Biff. "He's going back to Texas," Willy says sadly and incredulously. "What the hell's that?" Charley advises him dryly to let him go and forget about him. "You take it too hard," he says, "to hell with it." They continue to play cards, but the game soon ends as Willy becomes distracted by the ghostly appearance of his dead brother, Ben. He begins to address Charley as Ben, misdeals, and then accuses Charley of cheating. Charley leaves in a huff, and Willy begins to converse directly with the ghost.

Ben represents Willy's idea of success. He is the American dream, everything that Willy thinks he should have been himself. As Ben puts it, "When I was seventeen I walked into the jungle, and when I was twenty-one I walked out. And by God I was rich." Having made millions in the diamond business in Africa, and having left all seven of his children a handsome inheritance, Ben stands both as a model for Willy and as a constant reminder of his failure. In the imaginary scene that now transpires, Willy childishly attempts to gain Ben's approval, showing off his boys' athleticism and "manly" disregard for rules. He even boasts lamely that Brooklyn is not entirely unlike Africa—he and his boys hunt snakes and rabbits. Willy addresses Ben as a kind of oracle, asking him to tell Happy and Biff "how he did it." One again feels the terrible uncertainty and self-doubt beneath Willy's bluster as he pleads with Ben to stay longer and to advise him "how to teach" his boys. He admits to Ben that ever since their father died, he has felt "sort of temporary about [him]self." But Ben only retreats into a grandiose distance, saying he must get back to his many enterprises and repeating his pompous mantra about coming out of the jungle a rich man.

Willy's supplications to the departing ghost have led him out of the house. When Linda comes out to try to bring him inside, he insists on taking a walk, so she returns to the kitchen, where she is joined by Happy and Biff. For the first time, Linda candidly expresses to the boys the full depth of her worries about her husband, and the first act reaches its emotional peak. She tells the boys that Willy is trying to commit suicide. A witness to one of Willy's accidents has testified to an insurance inspector that she saw him deliberately turn his car into the railing of a bridge. And Linda herself has found a hole cut in one of the gas pipes in the basement and a length of rubber hose left there by Willy. She says that she takes the hose away every day, but then puts it back before Willy comes home because she is too "ashamed" to confront him.

His boss has taken away his salary, she explains, so that he only earns what he makes on commission, and she knows that this is not enough because he borrows money from Charley every week in order to maintain the pretense of sufficiency. He is not crazy, she says with tears in her voice, he is "exhausted"—"a small man can be just as exhausted as a great man." Worst of all, the children who were his reason for living have turned their backs on him. "Attention must be paid," she insists with great feeling, "attention must be paid to such a man." She appeals particularly to Biff: "His life is in your hands. . . ."

Biff and Happy are shocked and moved by what their mother tells them. Biff agrees to come home permanently, to make an earnest try at a business career, and to give half his paycheck to his father. Happy promises to settle down and get married, and comes up with an optimistic plan for a "Loman Brothers" sporting goods enterprise. Willy is greatly buoyed by their optimistic tone when he comes back into the house, and he goes to bed with high hopes, recalling the glorious day when Biff led his high school football team onto Ebbets Field, waving at his father in the audience. The first act ends with Biff going down into the basement, taking the rubber tube from behind the radiator, wrapping it around his hand, and going up the stairs.

Act 2 revolves around several meetings the following day—Biff's with Bill Oliver, Willy's with his young boss, then with Charley and Bernard, and later that evening with Biff and Happy in a restaurant for dinner. We do not actually see Biff's meeting with Bill Oliver, but we find out later that it has been a complete disaster. Bill Oliver does not remember Biff at all, and Biff steals his fountain pen when he steps out of the office. Willy's meeting with Howard is fully dramatized, but it is also a disaster. Howard refuses Willy's request to be transferred to a floor job. When Willy begins to harangue him in a raised voice—"You can't eat the orange and throw the fruit away, a man is not a piece of fruit!"—Howard fires him outright. Willy appeals to promises made by Howard's father, to friendship and familiarity, and to his many years of loyal service to the company. But Howard can only suggest with unintended irony that his two "wonderful" sons should be able to support him.

The next meeting is sad rather than bitter. After a brief interlude where Willy regretfully remembers Linda's resistance when his brother Ben tried to persuade him to go to Alaska, and another flashback to the day of Biff's appearance in Ebbets Field—"the greatest day of my life"—he takes himself to Charley's office to ask once again for a loan. In the sitting room he runs into Charley's son Bernard, who is on his way to Washington, we find out later, to try a case in front of the Supreme Court. Willy talks earnestly to Bernard, expressing his admiration of him and asking him where Biff went wrong. "He never trained himself for anything," the successful young lawyer says sincerely. Thinking back, Bernard recalls that he genuinely looked up to Biff when they were boys, but that for some inexplicable reason Biff seemed to lose the will to make something of himself after he failed math his senior year in high school. All he needed to do was make up the course in summer school, but after taking a trip to Boston to see you, Bernard says to Willy, he came back and quit altogether. He burnt the sneakers that had University of Virginia written on them, he fought with his friends, and I knew, Bernard says, that he had given up his life. "Did you tell him not to go to summer school?" Bernard asks. Willy becomes extremely defensive in response, and when Charley walks in Bernard pursues the question no further. Bernard takes his leave shortly thereafter, leaving Willy the chance to admit to Charley that he has been fired and once again to ask him for a loan. Charley gives him money, and once again offers him a job, which Willy again rejects. Though angered, Charley responds perceptively to Willy's dark suggestion that he is "worth more dead than alive." "Nobody's worth nothin dead," Charley says flatly. Willy is nearly in tears as he leaves, and for the first time he gives up pretending to be the "well-liked" salesman. "Charley," he says, "you're the only friend I got. Isn't that a remarkable thing?"

The final meeting, and the bulk of the second act, takes place in a restaurant where the boys have arranged to meet Willy at the end of the day. Happy arrives first and immediately begins flirting with a woman seated by herself nearby. By the time Biff arrives, Happy has caught the woman's interest. He tells her that Biff is a famous football star, and she goes off to cancel her date and to invite another female friend. Biff tells Happy of his fruitless "meeting" with Bill Oliver. "He gave me one look, and I realized what a ridiculous lie my whole life has been." He was never a salesman for Bill Oliver; he was a stock clerk. His father's need to believe in his son's imminent greatness was so relentless that Biff came to believe his fictions himself. But now he is determined to be honest—with himself and with his father. Happy tries to dissuade Biff from telling Willy about stealing the fountain pen, but Biff's mind is made up. When Willy arrives, Biff orders double scotches and begins to try to level with him. Willy, however, refuses to hear Biff out. As Biff speaks Willy continually manages to alter the story to accord with his own idealized expectations. When Biff insists on being heard, Willy blurts out the result of his own meeting: "I'm not interested in stories about the past or any crap of that kind because the woods are burning, boys, you understand? There's a big blaze going on all around. I was fired today." Shocked, Biff still persists in trying to tell his story accurately. But now Willy begins to lose contact with the present altogether. He fades into a long memory of the night Biff came to Boston to tell him that he had flunked math and found him with another woman. As the scene is played out on stage, with Biff sitting on the hotel bed crying, calling his father "a fake" and Willy trying lamely to explain, the audience learns finally the source of Biff's demoralization. Willy only comes back into the present long enough to insist impossibly that Biff go to lunch with Bill Oliver the next day, and to hit him for "spiting" his father. He leaves for the bathroom in a state of complete disorientation, and Happy and Biff leave with the girl Happy had flirted with and her friend.

"You're a pair of animals!" Linda shouts when the boys return home late that night to find her sitting alone with Willy's coat in her lap. In a dazed state, he has gone outside to try to plant seeds in the garden. "Not one, not another living soul," Linda continues, "would have had the cruelty to walk out on that man in a restaurant!" Biff self-hatingly admits to all her charges. He insists nonetheless that he must talk to his father and, against his mother's wishes, he finds Willy in the garden, fussing with seed packets and carrying on an imaginary conversation with his brother Ben about how well his wife and son might do with twenty thousand dollars worth of life insurance money. Biff interrupts his reverie without understanding its content, telling Willy he has come to say good-bye. They go inside, and the play's climactic confrontation ensues. Insisting that his father will never "see what I am," Biff tells Willy he must leave. Willy curses him, accusing him of "cutting down his life for spite." Finally, Biff places the rubber tube on the table, and insists that for once the truth be told. He scorns Happy's pretensions to be an "assistant buyer," he reveals that the reason he had no address for three months was because he stole a suit in Kansas City and was put in jail, and admits that he "stole myself out of every good job since high school." It is time to "say who I am," he says to Willy. "I'm a dime a dozen, and so are you. I'm a dollar an hour. I'm nothing! I'm nothing! No spite. I'm just what I am, that's all." He breaks down, crying. "Take that phony dream and burn it, before something happens."

Willy's response to Biff's breakdown is odd, poignant, and tragically characteristic. He is greatly gladdened by the evidence that Biff actually cares about him. "Isn't that remarkable?" he says, "Biff—he likes me! He cried! Cried to me. That boy is going to be magnificent." It is with the still bright hopes of contributing to this magnificence that he resists Linda's appeals to come to bed, instead going out and getting into his car. Biff and Linda hear the car squeal off and know immediately that they have seen Willy alive for the last time.

The final scene is a formal requiem, in which the characters gather in mourning dress, and each have their say about the death of the salesman. Happy is characteristically defiant and angry, promising to maintain Willy's dream and his fight. Charley is characteristically generous: "Nobody dast blame this man," he says forgivingly. Biff provides what is perhaps the play's final assessment of Willy's tragedy: "He didn't know himself." And Linda strikes a final note of lyricism and bitter irony. "We're free and clear," she says to Willy, speaking literally of having made the final payments of their mortgage, but figuratively of his release from suffering. "We're free and clear." The audience is left with the powerful and complex feelings that great literature often elicits toward its richest characters. We feel pity, and perhaps some contempt, for Willy Loman's weaknesses. We feel affection for his underlying decency and his desperate love of his family. And we feel frightened that we may share his illusions. ✤

—*Neal Dolan*
Harvard University

List of Characters

Willy Loman is the central figure of the play. An untalented but energetic man gripped by the American dream, Willy's personality disintegrates as he moves into his sixties and his strength begins to fail him. He commits suicide in the hopes of earning twenty thousand dollars in life insurance money for his wife and two grown sons. Over the course of the play, he is presented as a complex person who hides deep insecurity beneath a great deal of bluster and drive, relying on his handsome and athletic sons to compensate for his own sense of inadequacy. His willful hopefulness and exaggerated expectations betray him in the end by rendering him incapable of accepting himself or his children for who they are.

Linda is Willy's wife. She is a voice of wisdom and compassion in the play. She sees the many flaws and weaknesses of Willy and her sons but nonetheless loves them sincerely. She figures out early on that Willy is trying to kill himself, and she appeals to Biff, her older son, to try to help him. Her speech demanding that "attention must be paid" to Willy is one of the most emotionally powerful moments in American drama.

Biff is the older of Willy's two sons, and his favorite. Handsome and athletic, Biff was a popular and promising high school student who won football scholarships to three colleges. But the discovery that his father had a mistress demoralized him, and he never attended the summer school class required to complete high school. He tried briefly to build a career in business, but he found it demeaning and subsequently drifted from job to job out West. He reveals to Willy toward the end of the play that he recently spent time in jail for stealing a suit, and that he has in fact "stolen himself out of" every job he has had since high school. He blames Willy for giving him an inflated sense of self-importance, and he harbors deep anger at Willy for betraying his mother. He nonetheless loves his father intensely, and Willy's realization of this gives an oddly happy twist to his final decision to kill himself.

Happy is the younger of Willy's two sons. Like Biff, he is athletic and good-looking, but unlike Biff, he is a moderately successful businessman and a very successful womanizer. He confesses to having seduced the wives and fiancées of several of his bosses, and he is determined to prove himself in the business world. He cares deeply for his father but would rather indulge his illusions than attempt to tell him the truth as Biff does.

Charley is a neighbor of the Loman family. Despite Willy's impatient and frequently derisive attitude toward him, Charley intuits the extremity of Willy's situation. He attempts to help by offering Willy a job, but Willy refuses him on several occasions. His wry balance and objectivity present a stark contrast to Willy's mercurial intensity.

Bernard is Charley's son. As a studious high school student, he looked up to the athletic and magnetic Biff and attempted to help him on his exams. Biff, as well as Willy, looked down on him at the time, but they later envy him when he grows up to become a successful lawyer and a happy father.

Ben is Willy's brother who has died not long before the play begins. Having made a large fortune in the diamond business in Africa, he was successful in all the ways that Willy believes he himself should have been. At several points in the play, Willy addresses Ben as a kind of ghostly oracle, asking him for advice about what to tell his sons, or on how to be successful. ❖

Critical Views

[John Mason Brown (1900–1969) was a longtime the-atre reviewer for the *New York Post, Saturday Review,* and other periodicals. His reviews were collected in many volumes, including *The Art of Playgoing* (1936), *Broadway in Review* (1940), and *Dramatis Personae* (1963). In this review of the Broadway production of *Death of a Salesman,* Brown testifies to the emotional power of the play, declaring it a modern tragedy of great relevance to the present day.]

How good the writing of this or that of Mr. Miller's individual scenes may be, I do not know. Nor do I really care. When hit in the face, you do not bother to count the knuckles which strike you. All that matters, all you remember, is the staggering impact of the blow. Mr. Miller's is a terrific wallop, as furious in its onslaught on the heart as on the head. His play is the most poignant statement of man as he must face himself to have come out of our theatre. It finds the stuffs of life so mixed with the stuffs of the stage that they become one and indivisible.

If the proper study of mankind is man, man's inescapable problem is himself—what he would like to be, what he is, what he is not, and yet what he must live and die with. These are the moving, everyday, all-inclusive subjects with which Mr. Miller deals in *Death of a Salesman.* He handles them unflinchingly, with enormous sympathy, with genuine imagination, and in a mood which neither the prose of his dialogue nor the reality of his probing can rob of its poetry. Moreover, he has the wisdom and the insight not to blame the "system," in Mr. Odets' fash-ion, for what are the inner frailties and shortcomings of the individual. His rightful concern is with the dilemmas which are timeless in the drama because they are timeless in life.

Mr. Miller's play is a tragedy modern and personal, not clas-sic and heroic. Its central figure is a little man sentenced to discover his smallness rather than a big man undone by his greatness. Although he happens to be a salesman tested and found wanting by his own very special crises, all of us sitting out front are bound to be shaken, long before the evening is over, by finding something of ourselves in him. 〈. . .〉

Although *Death of a Salesman* is set in the present, it finds time and space to include the past. It plays the agonies of the moment of collapse against the pleasures and sorrows of recollected episodes. Mr. Miller is interested in more than the life and fate of his central character. His scene seems to be Willy Loman's mind and heart no less than his home. What we see might just as well be what Willy Loman thinks, feels, fears, or remembers as what we see him doing. This gives the play a double and successful exposure in time. It makes possible the constant fusion of what has been and what is. It also enables it to achieve a greater reality by having been freed from the fetters of realism.

Once again Mr. Miller shows how fearless and perceptive an emotionalist he is. He writes boldly and brilliantly about the way in which we disappoint those we love by having disappointed ourselves. He knows the torment of family tensions, the compensations of friendship, and the heartbreak that goes with broken pride and lost confidence. He is aware of the loyalties, not blind but open-eyed, which are needed to support mortals in their loneliness. The anatomy of failure, the pathos of age, and the tragedy of those years when a life begins to slip down the hill it has labored to climb are subjects at which he excels.

The quality and intensity of his writing can perhaps best be suggested by letting Mr. Miller speak for himself, or rather by allowing his characters to speak for him, in a single scene, in fact, in the concluding one. It is then that Willy's wife, his two sons, and his old friend move away from Jo Mielziner's brilliantly simple and imaginative multiple setting, and advance to the footlights. It is then that Mr. Miller's words supply a scenery of their own. Willy Loman, the failure and suicide, has supposedly just been buried, and all of us are at his grave, including his wife who wants to cry but cannot and who keeps thinking that it is just as if he were off on another trip.

"You don't understand," says Willy's friend, defending Willy from one of his sons. "Willy was a salesman. And for a salesman, there is no rock bottom to the life. He don't put a bolt to a nut, he don't tell you the law or give you medicine. He's a man way out there in the blue, ridin' on a smile and a shoeshine. And when they start not smilin' back—that's an earthquake. And then you get yourself a couple spots on your hat, and you're finished. Nobody dast blame this man. A salesman is got to dream, boy. It comes with the territory."

—John Mason Brown, "Even as You and I," *Saturday Review of Literature,* 26 February 1949, pp. 31–32

ARTHUR MILLER ON THE GENESIS OF *DEATH OF A SALESMAN*

[Arthur Miller has written much on his own plays, but one of the most insightful of his comments on *Death of a Salesman* comes from the lengthy introduction to his *Collected Plays* (1957). Here, Miller explains how a series of images led to the writing of his play.]

The first image that occurred to me which was to result in *Death of a Salesman* was of an enormous face the height of the proscenium arch which would appear and then open up, and we would see the inside of a man's head. In fact, *The Inside of His Head* was the first title. It was conceived half in laughter, for the inside of his head was a mass of contradictions. The image was in direct opposition to the method of *All My Sons*—a method one might call linear or eventual in that one fact or incident creates the necessity for the next. The *Salesman* image was from the beginning absorbed with the concept that nothing in life comes "next" but that everything exists together and at the same time within us; that there is no past to be "brought forward" in a human being, but that he is his past at every moment and that the present is merely that which his past is capable of noticing and smelling and reacting to. ⟨. . .⟩

The play grew from simple images. From a little frame house on a street of little frame houses, which had once been loud with the noise of growing boys, and then was empty and silent and finally occupied by strangers. Strangers who could not know with what conquistadorial joy Willy and his boys had once re-shingled the roof. Now it was quiet in the house, and the wrong people in the beds.

It grew from images of futility—the cavernous Sunday afternoons polishing the car. Where is that car now? And the chamois cloths carefully washed and put up to dry, where are the chamois cloths?

And the endless, convoluted discussions, wonderments, arguments, belittlements, encouragements, fiery resolutions, abdications, returns, partings, voyages out and voyages back, tremendous opportunities and small, squeaking denouements—and all in the kitchen now occupied by strangers who cannot hear what the walls are saying.

The image of aging and so many of your friends already gone and strangers in the seats of the mighty who do not know you or your triumphs or your incredible value.

The image of the son's hard, public eye upon you, no longer swept by your myth, no longer rousable from his separateness, no longer knowing you have lived for him and have wept for him.

The image of ferocity when love has turned to something else and yet is there, is somewhere in the room if one could only find it.

The image of people turning into strangers who only evaluate one another.

Above all, perhaps, the image of a need greater than hunger or sex or thirst, a need to leave a thumbprint somewhere on the world. A need for immortality, and by admitting it, the knowing that one has carefully inscribed one's name on a cake of ice on a hot July day.

I sought the relatedness of all things by isolating their unrelatedness, a man superbly alone with his sense of not having touched, and finally knowing in his extremity that the love which had always been in the room unlocated was now found.

The image of a suicide so mixed in motive as to be unfathomable and yet demanding statement. Revenge was in it and a power of love, a victory in that it would bequeath a fortune to the living and a flight from emptiness. With it an image of peace at the final curtain, the peace that is between wars, the peace leaving the issues above ground and viable yet.

And always, throughout, the image of private man in a world full of strangers, a world that is not home nor even an open battleground but only galaxies of high promise over a fear of falling.

And the image of a man making something with his hands being a rock to touch and return to. "He was always so wonderful with his hands," says his wife over his grave, and I laughed when the line came, laughed with the artist-devil's laugh, for it had all come together in this line, she having been made by him though he did not know it or believe in it or receive it into himself. Only rank, height of power, the sense of having won he believed was real—the galaxy thrust up into the sky by projectors on the rooftops of the city he believed were real stars.

—Arthur Miller, "Introduction," *Collected Plays* (New York: Viking Press, 1957), pp. 23, 29–30

HERBERT J. MULLER ON THE TRAGEDY OF A "LITTLE MAN"

[Herbert J. Muller (b. 1905), Professor Emeritus at Indiana University, is a prolific critic and historian and author of such works as *Modern Fiction: A Study in Values* (1937), *The Uses of the Past* (1952), and *Freedom in the Modern World* (1966). In this extract, Muller shows how Miller's play differs from the standard tragedy by focusing on a man who clearly lacks greatness; but Muller criticizes Miller for investing the play with a grandeur that Willy Loman is unable to sustain.]

As the study of a little man succumbing to his environment, rather than a great man destroyed through his greatness,

⟨*Death of a Salesman*⟩ is characteristically modern. There is no question of grandeur in such a tragedy; the "hero" may excite pity, but nothing like awe. There is a question of dignity and human significance. While the dramatic reviewers were generally enthusiastic about the play as a heart-warming one, or even an "epic drama," the fastidious critics of the quarterlies generally dismissed it as a "very dull business," without illumination or pity, or a string of clichés of "unrelieved vulgarity." It strikes me as a basically humane, honest work. It gives some dignity to the tragedy of Willy by an at once unsparing and sympathetic treatment of his easy good nature, his passion to be well liked, his want of any mind or soul of his own. The pathetic Willy may even symbolize Everyman in the wider sense felt by John Mason Brown: "what he would like to be, what he is, what he is not, and yet what he must live and die with."

But Miller, too, strains for a "big" play. His supra-realistic effects—such as the expressionistic setting, the musical themes for the various characters, and the portentous apparitions of Brother Ben—are too fancy for little Willy, and seem more pretentious because of the flat colloquial dialogue. So do the occasional efforts to sound a deep note. "I search and search and I search, and I can't understand it, Willy," his wife laments over his grave; but throughout the play she has not been searching and has understood Willy well enough. Miller's own understanding of him, however, is unclear. Sometimes it appears that the main cause of his tragedy is capitalism; sometimes it is Babbittry, his own weaknesses; sometimes it is the universal plight of the Little Man. The uncertain intention has led to curiously divergent judgments of simple Willy. In England, Ivor Brown remarked, he was taken as "a poor, flashy, self-deceiving little man," whose passion for popularity was more contemptible than natural; the play was coolly received. In America, Brooks Atkinson described him as "a good man who represents the homely, decent, kindly virtues of a middle-class society"; Broadway audiences wept over him. Marxists might explain the tears shed by New Yorkers over his kind of failure, whom in real life they would despise, as a sentimental evasion of their responsibility for such failures. In any case, the excitement over Willy would seem to be more a social than a literary portent.

—Herbert J. Muller, *The Spirit of Tragedy* (New York: Knopf, 1957), pp. 316–17

LORRAINE HANSBERRY ON THE AMERICANISM OF *DEATH OF A SALESMAN*

[Lorraine Hansberry (1930–1965) was a leading black American playwright whose *A Raisin in the Sun* (1959), which won the New York Drama Critics Circle Award, was inspired by *Death of a Salesman*. In this extract, Hansberry believes Miller's play to be prototypically American in its setting and action.]

We knew who Willy Loman was instantaneously; we recognized his milieu. We also knew at once that he represented that curious paradox in what the *English* character in that *English* play could call, though dismally, "The American Age." Willy Loman was a product of a nation of great military strength, indescribable material wealth, and incredible mastery of the physical realm, which nonetheless was unable, in 1946, to produce a *typical* hero who was capable of an affirmative view of life.

I believe it is a testament to Miller's brilliance that it is hardly a misstatement of the case, as some preferred to believe. Something has indeed gone wrong with at least part of the American dream, and Willy Loman is the victim of the detour. Willy had to be overwhelmed on the stage as, in fact, his prototypes are in everyday life. Coming out of his section of our great sprawling middle class, preoccupied with its own restlessness and displaying its obsession for the possession of trivia, Willy was indeed trapped. His predicament in a New World where there just aren't anymore forests to clear or virgin railroads to lay or native American empires to first steal and then build upon left him with nothing but some left-over values which had forgotten how to prize industriousness over cunning, usefulness over mere acquisition, and above all, humanism over "success." The potency of the great tale of a salesman's death was in our familiar recognition of his entrapment which, suicide or no, is *deathly*.

—Lorraine Hansberry, "An Author's Reflections: Willy Loman, Walter Younger, and He Who Must Live," *Village Voice,* 12 August 1959, p. 7

Henry Popkin on Willy Loman as an Everyman

[Henry Popkin is a professor of English at the State University of New York at Buffalo and has produced an edition of Oscar Wilde's *The Importance of Being Earnest* (1965). In this extract, Popkin studies Willy Loman as an Everyman figure, showing how *Death of a Salesman* belongs to the tradition of Expressionism.]

Willy is much more emphatically a representative figure, an American Everyman, than any of Miller's other characters; accordingly, his problems are much less personal dilemmas than they are public issues. Willy is a useful instrument for Miller's social criticism. This quality of his is the first trait by which we identify this play as an example of Expressionism. Certainly this concern with large social issues is the key to Miller's definition of Expressionism in his Harvard lecture ("The Family in Modern Drama," *Atlantic Monthly,* April 1956): "It is a form . . . which manifestly seeks to dramatize the conflict of either social, religious, or moral forces *per se.*" In his most recent article, Miller finds that the Greeks and the Expressionists are alike in their effort "to present the hidden forces."

The hallmarks of Expressionism are its employment of symbolic characters—The Man, the Woman, the Nameless One (all three in Ernst Toller's *Man and the Masses),* Elmer Rice's Mr. Zero, Miller's Loman—and its presentation of dream states in which hidden forces of every variety become plainly visible. It was against the pioneer Expressionist, August Strindberg, that Zola lodged the complaint that he did not know the last names of the characters in *The Father;* the characters of this play are like Miller's Charley and Bernard in this respect, but no one complained about Miller's rootless figures. Perhaps the audience took it for granted that their name was Everyman. Certainly the acquired taste for Expressionism has made headway since the first American experiments in the 1920's. This dramatic *genre* had been in vogue among *avant garde* audiences for half a century before Miller adopted it. What is new is its presence in a popular success of fabulous proportions. If Strindberg won the connoisseur's attention with *The Dream Play,* O'Neill with *The Hairy Ape,* and Elmer Rice with *The Adding Machine,* what popular fame these writers earned rested on other plays. But with *Death of a Salesman,* Expressionism descended, in a slightly watered-down form, to the mass audience.

The Everyman element is obvious enough. To locate the dream-elements of the play also requires no great effort. Willy Loman's dreams occupy half the play; they are the dreams of all the world, the dreams of a happy, hopeful past and the inescapable dream of past guilt. The recollections are not straight flashbacks in the manner of the films, but they are distorted, speeded up, heightened by repetition and selection. The accompanying music and the distinctive lighting of the original production compelled us to set these remembrances apart from objective reality. Further testimony of unreality is to be found in one figure who appears in them but seems to have no existence in the real world—Uncle Ben, the embodiment of the American will to succeed. He is the fantastically rich relative who shuttles between the outposts of imperialism, Alaska and Africa. Long ago, he set out for Alaska to dig gold; he found himself on the way to Africa instead, and so he made his fortune in diamonds. When Willy last sees him, he is heading for Alaska. During the dream sequences, Willy seems unable to tell truth from fantasy, the present from the past. He loses himself in his recollections, interrupting a conversation with his neighbor Charley to address the absent Ben, losing all sense of the present in a men's room while he recalls his past exposure by his son. Willy is sick; his mental breakdown is certified by the hold his recollections have on him and by the great amount of obvious distortion in them. He has symptoms of schizophrenia, but his sickness is not his alone. His identification with Everyman assures us that, as in other Expressionist plays, we are examining the malady not of an individual but of society.

—Henry Popkin, "Arthur Miller: The Strange Encounter," *Sewanee Review* 68, No. 1 (Winter 1960): 50–52

LEONARD MOSS ON WILLY LOMAN'S SPEECH

[Leonard Moss (b. 1931) is the author of *Arthur Miller* (1967; rev. 1980). In this extract, Moss studies Willy Loman's speech, believing that his words offer a clear portrait of his own superficiality and moral immaturity.]

Willy Loman characterizes himself by the manner in which he speaks. "Well, bottoms up! . . . And keep your pores open!" he crudely reminds his extracurricular girlfriend, in tasteless cant of the thirties. When he gropes for metaphoric originality he cannot escape staleness: "Because you got a greatness in you, Biff, remember that . . . Like a young God. Hercules—something like that. And the sun, the sun all around him." His most pathetic laments are stock phrases: "Where are you guys, where are you?" he calls to his sons, "The woods are burning!"

Willy indicates his superficiality through hackneyed catchwords that advertise a business ethic based on "personal attractiveness." "Because the man who makes an appearance in the business world, the man who creates personal interest, is the man who gets ahead," he pontificates, in an aphoristic rhythm; "Be liked and you will never want." Childlike, he gains assurance by repeating his facile success formulas: "It's not what you do, Ben. It's who you know and the smile on your face! It's contacts, Ben, contacts! The whole wealth of Alaska passes over the lunch table at the Commodore Hotel, and that's the wonder, the wonder of this country, that a man can end with diamonds here on the basis of being liked!" (His wife and younger son echo the favorite magical cliché; Hap's compliment to Biff is "you're well liked," and Linda asks, "Why must everybody conquer the world? You're well liked.") Stressing the potent terms, Willy explains, "I realized that selling was the greatest career a man could want . . . there was personality in it, Howard. There was respect, and comradeship, and gratitude in it." Even his sons' names—Happy and Biff—reflect his naive euphoria.

The Salesman suggests his moral immaturity and confusion in another way through his many self-contradictions when offering advice to Biff. Though he warns that " 'Gee' is a boy's word," he uses the term frequently. He shouts at his son, "Not finding yourself at the age of thirty-four is a disgrace!" but later adds, "Greatest thing in the world for him to bum around." "Biff is a lazy bum," he grumbles; then, "And such a hard worker. There's one thing about Biff—he's not lazy." He gives this advice before the interview with Oliver: "Walk in very serious. You are not applying for a boy's job. Money is to pass. Be quiet, fine, and serious. Everybody likes a kidder, but nobody lends him money." A few lines after he cautions, "Walk in with a big laugh. Don't look worried. Start off with a couple of your good stories to lighten things up. It's not what you say, it's how you say it—because personality always wins the day." Memories of past conversations reproduce similar inconsistencies. He excused Biff's stealing a football from the school locker room: "Sure, he's gotta practice with a regulation ball, doesn't he? Coach'll probably congratulate you on your initiative!" Yet he soon forgot this excuse: "He's giving it back, isn't he? Why is he stealing? What did I tell him? I never in my life told him anything but decent things." ("Why am I always being contradicted?" he wonders.)

Still other techniques could be cited, particularly the associations operative in Willy's nightmarish recollections, but enough has been said to make the point that Miller's dialogue is most telling when it works by implication rather than by explication.

—Leonard Moss, "Arthur Miller and the Common Man's Language," *Modern Drama* 7, No. 1 (Summer 1964): 55–56

[Arthur K. Oberg (1938–1977) was a professor of English at the University of Washington. Among his books are a critical study, *Modern American Lyric* (1978), and a collection of poetry, *Anna's Song* (1980). In this extract, Oberg shows how the dialogue in *Death of a Salesman* is characteristic of Miller's entire work.]

From Miller's earliest plays to *Incident at Vichy* there is a distinctive speech which, regardless of ostensible setting or background of characters, is based upon a New York idiom that often has recognizably Jewish inflection (e.g. the rising rhythms of "Does it take more guts to stand here the rest of my life ringing up a zero?"). Miller has an ear for speech that can be heard in any of the New York boroughs, for rhythms that have filtered down into Gentile conversation many miles from the city. Beginning with a particular speech, Miller arrives at something that approaches an American idiom to the extent that it exposes a colloquialism characterized by unusual image, spurious lyricism, and close-ended cliché. One has the impression of characters cheering themselves up with speech that is counterpointed by what we already know as audience about them. For Miller, it is a conscious selection from the speech that he has known and heard from childhood through which he exposes such discrepancies, particularly rents in the American dream. And it is in *Death of a Salesman* that he perfects this idiom to allow for a more successful revelation of complex character than in any other play he wrote.

The language of *Death of a Salesman* has characteristics that link it with all of Miller's work. Miller has a talent for using words and phrases as leitmotifs ("He's liked, but he's not—well liked"), for writing what approaches but is less obvious and shorter than set speech. Linda and Willy's occasional soliloquy-like musings relate to the kind of patterned speech that typifies Miller's earlier and later plays:

> The cats in that alley are practical, the bums who ran away when we were fighting were practical. Only the dead ones weren't practical. But now I'm practical, and I spit on myself. I'm going away. I'm going now. (*All My Sons*)

> No, no. Now let me instruct you. We cannot look to superstition in this. The Devil is precise; the marks of his presence are definite as stone, and I must tell you all that I shall not proceed unless you are prepared to believe me if I should find no bruise of hell upon her. (*The Crucible*)

Similarly, prominent striking images ("He was so humiliated he nearly limped when he came in"; "All the talk that went across those two beds, huh? Our whole lives," recall the earmarks of other plays, dialogue that hesitates between mixed metaphor and metaphysical conceit:

> Frank is right—every man does have a star. The star of one's honesty. (*All My Sons*)

> This society will not be a bag to swing around your head, Mr. Putnam. (*The Crucible*)

> Quentin, don't hold the future like a vase—touch now, touch me! I'm here, and it's now! (*After the Fall*)

> You'd better ram a viewpoint up your spine or you'll break in half. (*Incident at Vichy*)

Miller here reveals three things: a knack of linking an abstract and a concrete in metaphor, a pressing of metaphor to visual incongruity or cartoon-like animation, and a preference for letting an audience bear away one or two vivid images in contrast to the *copia* of a playwright like Christopher Fry. While implicit attitudes toward kinds of rhetoric possible within a contemporary play would further link *Death of a Salesman* with the body of Miller's work, it is the particular density of a familiar Miller rhetoric that gives *Death of a Salesman* a feel that none of his other plays achieves. And the density is dictated by the enclosed situation in which the main character is found.

When Miller undertook in *Death of a Salesman* to present the plight of Willy Loman, he offered a reexamination of radical aspects of the American dream. The Lomans, never a family of adults, gradually and painfully attest to discrepancies in the American success myth, discrepancies that their lives from time to time can no longer hide. What Willy and his sons and what Charley and Bernard indicate in their respective failures and successes is the presence of arbitrary gods. Willy clings to them as he is beaten by them, and Miller's "requiem" confirms them as a part of the territory. For Loman, they are both equipment for living and vestments of death. As the play moves through its rhythms of euphoric elation and relentless despair, Miller employs a speech that would uphold these values by embedding them in outworn, formulated clichés commonly negatively phrased: "Never fight fair with a stranger, boy," "nobody's worth nothin' dead," "No man only needs a little salary." But elsewhere there is language that draws near to "something of a poetic tinge," "a great air of something like poetry," "a kind of poetry":

> The world is an oyster, but you don't crack it open on a mattress!

> When a deposit bottle is broken you don't get your nickel back.

> Everybody likes a kidder, but nobody lends him money.

But even when Miller attempts to revitalize language we detect one and the same process here going on—the reduction of living to a set of adages, whether familiar or not.

—Arthur K. Oberg, "*Death of a Salesman* and Arthur Miller's Search for Style," *Criticism* 9, No. 4 (Fall 1967): 305–8

THOMAS E. PORTER ON LINDA LOMAN

[Thomas E. Porter (b. 1928) is a former professor of English at the University of Detroit and the author of *Myth and Modern American Drama* (1969), from which the following extract is taken. Here, Porter examines the figure of Willy Loman's wife, Linda, believing that her very acceptance of Willy's conception of the world helps to bring about his downfall.]

Linda is the heart of the family. She is wise, warm, sympathetic. She knows her husband's faults and her sons' characters. For all her frank appraisals, she loves them. She is contrasted with the promiscuous sex symbolized by the Woman and the prostitutes. They operate in the world outside as part of the impersonal forces that corrupt. Happy equates his promiscuity with taking manufacturers' bribes, and Willy's Boston woman can "put him right through to the buyers." Linda holds the family together—she keeps the accounts, encourages her husband, tries to protect him from heartbreak. She becomes the personi- fication of Family, that social unity in which the individual has a real identity.

> The concepts of Father and Mother and so on were received by us unawares before the time we were conscious of ourselves as selves. In contrast, the concepts of Friend, Teacher, Employee, Boss, Colleague, Supervisor, and the many other social relations come to us long after we have gained consciousness of our- selves, and are therefore outside ourselves. They are thus in an objective rather than a subjective category. In any case what we feel is always more "real" to us than what we know, and we feel the family relationship while we only know the social one. (Arthur Miller, "The Family in Modern Drama")

If Willy is not totally unsympathetic (and he is not), much of the goodness in him is demonstrated in his devotion to his wife, according to his lights. Though he is often masterful and curt, he is still deeply concerned about her: "I was fired, and I'm looking for a little good news to tell your mother, because the woman has waited and the woman has suffered." Biff is attached to his mother, and Happy's hopelessness is most graphic in his failure to be honest with, or concerned about, his family. The family's devotion to one another, even though mis- guided, represents a recognizable American ideal.

Linda, for all her warmth and goodness, goes along with her husband and sons in the best success-manual tradition. She tries to protect them from the forces outside and fails. The memory of her suffering and her fidelity does not keep Willy and Happy from sex or Biff from wandering. Miller's irony goes still deeper. While Linda is a mirror of goodness and the source of the family's sense of identity, she is no protection—by her silence and her support, she unwittingly cooperates with the destructive myth. Linda follows the rules laid down by the self- help advocates. She is a good home manager, she understands and encourages her husband, she keeps her house neat and is a good mother. Babson recommends a good wife as a major factor in working toward success: "A good wife and well-kept house and some healthy children are of the utmost importance in enabling one to develop the six 'I's' of success and to live the normal, wholesome, upright life." Linda stays in her place, never questioning out loud her husband's objectives and doing her part to help him achieve them.

—Thomas E. Porter, "Acres of Diamonds: *Death of a Salesman*," *Myth and Modern American Drama* (Detroit: Wayne State University Press, 1969), pp. 146–47

❖

JOHN VON SZELISKI ON WILLY LOMAN'S MATERIAL VALUES

[John von Szeliski (b. 1934) is a former professor of drama at Williams College and the author of *Tragedy and Fear: Why Modern Tragic Drama Fails* (1971), from which the following extract is taken. Here, von Szeliski maintains that Willy Loman's failure derives from the fact that his values are not in fact moral but merely material, reflecting the materialism of society as a whole.]

Part of the atmosphere of perennial defeat in this household comes from the impersonality of the automated, mechanized society that has substituted mass mediocrity for slowly cultured quality. The Lomans know intimately the seemingly petty defeats of broken-down refrigerators, carburetor trouble, and the like. At the same time, they respond, with all "common" men ("common" by the advertising industry's definition of mass attraction) to the mass-production values. Willy himself, as a salesman, must represent those values to the consumer. Willy and Linda can leak out their earnings for a mountain of minor repairs, and then justify their decision to purchase a particular brand by saying: "They had the biggest ads of any of them!" Miller's comment in another interview points to another aspect of such adopted values; "Willy is a victim; he didn't originate this thing. He believes that selling is the greatest thing anybody can do."

Miller says he was careful not to inject a personal statement of his philosophy into the play. Yet Willy is so obviously wrong in all he does, all the while "meaning well" and loving his family, that a statement of values seems especially needed. We only see a world which is mutually infected by Willy's helplessly perverted dreams and codes. If the characters are deliberately and pessimistically drawn as limited intelligences, there can be little perspective on values from within the play. Could Linda be a source? She seems most sensible and most objective, but she has a policy of single-minded support of Willy. Her love is then impressive but her values routine.

Willy's self-building only develops the ground for his later paranoia, when he decides the world has treated him badly in the light of his greatness *as he imagined it:*

> And they know me, boys, they know me up and down New England. The finest people. And when I bring you fellas up, there'll be open sesame for all of us, 'cause one thing, boys: I have friends. I can park my car in any street in New England, and the cops protect it like their own.

Thus the Loman men feed on each other's empty values, resulting in their eventual cynicism about modern life in the city: eat, sleep, work, and then more of the same. Lack of values means lack of ethic plus lack of knowledge. The result: pessimism and cynicism. Eventually Biff vaguely wants to marry "somebody with character, with resistance:" that is, both Happy and Biff agree they must seek someone to challenge them as Linda and Willy have not.

The object of Willy's code is understandable. He's got a poignant dream and we can sympathize with it. We all desire recognition, and we want him to have it, wrong and false though he may be. He will share it with his family, too. But his means to this object remain at least amoral if not immoral. While Miller naturally criticizes Willy, it is nonetheless clear that Willy is Miller's (and our) pathos-object. It is sad what was expedient to the Lomans, but this is not a moral statement, even though Miller is normally one of our more moral playwrights.

Willy's dangerous thinking, forced on him by society, is also somewhat inherited, and Willy in turn will pass this on to Biff, and Biff would pass it on to his children. Willy's brother Ben says to Biff what is probably the same thing Willy heard from his father years ago: "Never fight fair with a stranger, boy. You'll never get out of the jungle that way." There are two interesting suppositions here: that they *are* in a jungle, and that one must force one's way out. They are keystones of the Loman pessimism, and ironically Willy is not aware enough to be a fighter. These only explain and do not justify Willy's perennial defensiveness. The main conclusion is that those who get out of the jungle are the treacherous battlers and connivers and thus the earth is inherited by some cross between rats and apes. Accordingly, Ben's repeated boast that he was rich at seventeen is Willy's favorite piece of literature: "That's just the spirit I want to imbue them with! To walk into a jungle! I was right! I was right! I was right!"

So Willy is destroyed by his values, and they are not moral or ethical values, but situational and material codes. They alienate Biff even as Biff learns of no alternative to this type of value. That is Willy's greatest loss and the final impetus for suicide. Simply put, Willy is a professional failure. His values wouldn't matter to the company if only he could maintain his quota and not act so strangely.

Death of a Salesman, for all its excellence as a drama, then shares the typical weaknesses of the other pessimistic plays when it comes to moral statement. Nothing has been said distinctly or strongly in any of the areas that might pass for such statement—not on sin, or error, or moral belief, or mere common-sense values. But even this is not the ultimate problem with the pessimistic would-be tragedy. It is finally a matter of enlightenment.

—John von Szeliski, Tragedy and Fear: Why Modern Tragic Drama Fails (Chapel Hill: University of North Carolina Press, 1971), pp. 163–65

STANLEY KAUFFMANN ON THE FAILINGS OF *DEATH OF A SALESMAN*

[Stanley Kauffmann (b. 1916) was a longtime theatre and film critic for the *New Republic* and *Saturday*

Review. His reviews have been collected in many volumes, including *A World on Film* (1966), *Persons of the Drama* (1976), and *Distinguishing Features* (1994). In this extract, Kauffmann delivers a harsh criticism on many features of *Death of a Salesman,* from its diction to its theme to several features of its plot.]

⟨. . .⟩ to see the play again is to see how Arthur Miller lacked the control and vision to fulfill his own idea. First consider the diction of the play, because a play is its language, first and finally. *Salesman* falters badly in this regard. At its best, its true and telling best, the diction is first-generation Brooklyn Jewish. ("Attention, attention must be finally paid to such a person.") But often the dialogue slips into a fanciness that is slightly ludicrous. To hear Biff say, "I've been remiss," to hear Linda say, "He was crestfallen, Willy" is like watching a car run off the road momentarily onto the shoulder. (I've never heard anyone use the word "crestfallen" in my life.) Then there is the language of Willy's brother Ben, the apparition of piratical success. He speaks like nothing but a symbol, and not a symbol connected with Willy in any perceptible way. Miller *says* he's Willy's brother, that's all. The very use of diamonds as the source of Ben's wealth has an almost childishly symbolic quality about it. When Miller's language is close to the stenographic, the remembered, it's good; otherwise, it tends to literary juvenility, a pretended return from pretended experience.

Thematically, too, the play is cloudy. It's hard to believe that, centrally, Miller had anything more than muzzy anti-business, anti-technology impulses in his head. Is Willy a man shattered by business failure and by disappointment in his sons? Then why, when he is younger and at least making a living, when he is proud of his sons and they of him, does he lie about his earnings to Linda and then have to correct himself? Why, at the peak of his life, does he undercut his own four-flushing to tell her that people don't take to him, that they laugh at him? The figure that comes through the play is not of a man brought down by various failures but of a mentally unstable man in whom the fissures have increased. Willy is shown to be at least as much a victim of psychopathy as of the bitch goddess. When was he ever rational or dependable? Is this a tragedy of belief in the American romance or the end of a clinical case?

43

But assume, for argument, that Willy is not a psychopath, that he was a relatively whole man now crushed by the American juggernaut. What is the play's attitude toward that juggernaut, toward business ideals? There is no anagnorisis for Willy, no moment of recognition: he dies believing in money—in fact, he kills himself for it, to give his son Biff the insurance benefit as a stake for more business. His son Happy is wedded to money values and says over his father's coffin that he's going to stick to them for his father's sake. Biff was so aggrandized by his father that he became kleptomaniacal as a boy and even now, after his father-as-idol has collapsed, can't resist stealing a successful man's fountain pen as a niggling vindictiveness against that man's success and his own non-success. The only alternatives to the business ethos ever produced in the play are Willy's love of tools and seeds, building and planting, and Biff's love of outdoor life. As between romances, I'll take business.

Miller confuses matters even further by the success of young Bernard next door as a lawyer in the Establishment world, a success for which Willy feels envy. What we are left with is neither a critique of the business world nor an adult vision of something different and better, but the story of a man (granting he was sane) who failed, as salesman and father, and who made things worse by refusing to the end to admit those failures, which he knew were true. That is one play, and possibly a good one if it were realized; but it is quite a different one from a play that, in its atmosphere and mannerisms, implies radical perception about deep American ills.

Some other points. When I saw the film in 1952, which made the environment more vivid, I couldn't help wondering why Willy had money worries: he had almost paid off the mortgage on his house, which was a piece of real estate in an increasingly valuable and desirable section, to judge by the building going on all around it. I don't think this is a petty literal point in a realistic play whose lexicon is bill-paying. Further, all the dialogue about Willy's father, with his wagon-travels through the West and his flutes, seems falser than ever, Miller's imposition on this Brooklyn play to give it historical base and continental sweep. As with the character of Ben, there is a schism in tenor between this material and the rest of the play.

Last, a point that is strangely more apparent now than it was in 1949 when *Salesman* first appeared: the play is set in the late 1940s and reaches back some fifteen years, yet there is scarcely a mention of World War II. How did Biff and Happy escape it? If they didn't, wouldn't the reunited brothers have had something to say about it? And wouldn't the war have had some effect on Willy's past-cum-present view of promise-crammed America?

Some of the play is touching still: Willy when he is at his most salesman-like, the Requiem over his coffin, and much of the material on Miller's favorite theme, the love-hate of father and son. But these are sound moments in a flabby, occasionally false work. Miller had gift enough to get the idea, but then settled for the dynamics of the idea itself, supported by a vague high-mindedness, to write his play for him. As the world knows, many viewers and readers have taken the intent for the deed. Some have not. And for one viewer this new production only emphasizes the gap between intent and accomplishment.

—Stanley Kauffmann, "Death of a Salesman" (1976), *Persons of the Drama* (New York: Harper & Row, 1976), pp. 143–45

ROBERT N. WILSON ON *DEATH OF A SALESMAN* AS AN INDICTMENT OF THE AMERICAN DREAM

[Robert N. Wilson (b. 1924) is the author of many critical studies, including *Man Made Plain: The Poet in Contemporary Society* (1958), *Experiencing Creativity: On the Social Psychology of Art* (1986), and *The American Poet: A Role Investigation* (1990). In this extract, Wilson maintains that the play lays bare the shallowness and cruelty of the American dream of success as tied to monetary gain and social standing.]

Willy with his sample cases is not only the father, with his burdensome sons, parental responsibilities, and vast vulnerabilities. He is also, and as importantly, a salesman sui generis. Those cases straining his arms and seeming to drain him of vitality are not merely symbols; they contain real goods for sale, and Willy in trying to peddle them is a pathetic archetype of the American dream of success. Despite the fact that most Americans are not salesmen by a strict occupational definition, that, unlike Willy, we work in large organizations and are hourly or salaried employees, we have all of us something of the salesman and dream his dream of a success obtained through individual desire and energy. What Erich Fromm termed the "marketing orientation" is woven into the fabric of our national life; in this disposition of personality, the individual's credo is "I am as you desire me." So Willy attempts to be the person he thinks others desire: for his customers, the jovial yet dignified drummer; for his sons, the firm yet indulgent and all-protective father; for his wife, the ever-dependable breadwinner. He tells Biff and Happy about his friends: "And they know me, boys, they know me up and down New England. The finest people. And when I bring you fellas up, there'll be open sesame for all of us, 'cause one thing, boys: I have friends. I can park my car in any street in New England, and the cops protect it like their own." In this society we all feel, more or less keenly, that we must sell ourselves, must be responsive to the demands of others, must make a good impression in order to be (as Willy puts it) not just "liked, but *well* liked."

When we see *Death of a Salesman* we are truly "guilty creatures at a play." Willy's failure is our failure, for we are also involved in the cult of success, and we, too, measure men by occupational attainment rather than by some sympathetic calculus of the whole human being. We are all partners in the American Dream and parties to the conspiracy of silence surrounding the fact that failures must by definition outnumber successes, given our cultural ground rules and our singular interpretations of the words "success" and "failure." Surely part of the undeniable power Miller's play exerts is rooted in the author's audacity in breaking this conspiracy of silence, in revealing to us a failure almost too painful for audiences to bear. How many times has one heard contemporaries exclaim that Willy reminds them of their own fathers, and that they find a deep loving sorrow in the reminiscence. One of the master themes in twentieth-century American literature is the articulation of the individual's quest for a vocational identity and a satisfying public image of self with the private world of family relationships. O'Neill, Fitzgerald, Hemingway—all grapple with the devilish ambiguities and profound disappointments that seem intrinsic to the striving for success and its attendant lack of domestic tranquility.

—Robert N. Wilson, "The Salesman and Society," *The Writer as Social Seer* (Chapel Hill: University of North Carolina Press, 1979), pp. 59–61

ARTHUR GANZ ON *DEATH OF A SALESMAN* AS A FAILED CRITIQUE OF AMERICAN SOCIETY

[Arthur Ganz (b. 1928) is a professor of English at the City College of the City University of New York and author of *George Bernard Shaw* (1983). In this extract, from his earlier book, *Realms of the Self* (1980), Ganz finds that Miller's play does not present a coherent criticism of American society.]

If we set aside the play's structure and attempt to examine Willy's philosophy directly, similar problems arise. Willy is a man so foolish as to believe that success in the business world can be achieved not by work and ability but by being "well liked," by a kind of hearty popularity that will open all doors and provide favors and preferential treatment. So convinced is Willy of the rightness of his doctrine that he raises his sons by it and, without intending to, subtly undermines their moral character, turning one into a lecher and the other into a thief. If the death of Willy Loman is to be any more significant than the death of many another pathetic incompetent, and Miller clearly wishes it to be so, then Willy's doctrine, the ultimate cause of his downfall, must be both dangerous and widespread. When pushed to Willy's extreme, it is no doubt dangerous, but that it is widespread is doubtful. That many Americans are obsessed by the idea of commercial success is surely a truth, though hardly an original one; that large numbers of such persons intend to achieve their goals primarily by cultivating the art of camaraderie is most unlikely. We are, in other words, being elaborately warned against a danger that is not dangerous. Indeed, Willy's touching desire to be liked often strikes us as one of his most endearing characteristics. For all his bluster and his terrible incomprehension, we do like him. His death moves us, perhaps because he so obviously wanted us to be moved. The desire to be liked functions in the play emotionally, but intellectually it is meaningless. It is not at the root of the socioeconomic ills of modern American society, and a critique of that society based upon it would be entirely without validity. Yet a critique of some pretensions seems to be present in the play: if it is not based on Willy's doctrine, we may reasonably ask what it is based on.

Unfortunately, the question is more easily asked than answered, for the play, when closely examined, yields not one critique but at least three, each distinct and each negating the other. From one point of view, Miller's dissatisfaction with the society that Willy Loman exemplifies stems from an implicit comparison between it and a previous one that was stronger, simpler, and more noble. So considered, Willy's society is no more than the corruption of the pioneer vision of a pastoral edenic world peopled by a dignified race finding fulfillment in its labors. Willy, then, represents the degeneration of an older, stronger stock, described by his brother Ben:

> Father was a very great and a very wild-hearted man. We would start in Boston, and he'd toss the whole family into the wagon, and then he'd drive the team right across the country; through Ohio, and Indiana, Michigan, Illinois, and all the Western states. And we'd stop in the towns and sell the flutes that he'd made on the way. Great inventor, Father. With one gadget he made more in a week than a man like you could make in a lifetime.

Willy's father, too, was a salesman, but he was also a pioneer and sold the artistic products of his own hands. The end of this speech is colored by Ben's character, but even that character is ambiguous, for Ben's business in Alaska and his offer to Willy suggest the pioneer developer as much as the capitalist exploiter. It is this character of the hardy, simple man, happy in a rural environment (as the cowboys of *The Misfits* might have been happy) that Willy's dreams seem to have corrupted. Biff says that he and his brother should work outdoors; Willy is never happier than when doing manual work about the house. But this life is not possible. Brooklyn is no longer a place where one can hunt rabbits (again, a hint of the lost Eden) but a place where the few anachronistic houses like Willy's are ringed by the characterless apartment buildings of an industrial-commercial civilization. Dave Singleman, the eighty-four-year-old salesman upon whom Willy had modeled himself, derived respect and friendship from his work, but Willy is alone in a world that ignores him.

If the central motive of this play is a critique of American society as the corrupted remnant of a great pioneer vision, then Willy has much to answer for. If the thousands of Willys whom Miller evidently finds in our society have through their stupidity and vulgarity destroyed the rustic happiness that Miller appears to see in the American past, then they are guilty of a great crime and deserve their fates. But Miller does not seem to condemn Willy, at least not very forcefully, for there is a strong suggestion that his fate has been thrust upon him by forces beyond his control or indeed his comprehension. The pathetic picture of the tired old salesman, helpless in an over-whelming environment, does not suggest the righteous destruction of the wicked. There are other men in the play far worse than Willy. The speech about Willy's pioneer-flutist father is delivered by Ben (no one else is available to give it), but he is a very different sort of person. Ben presents his philosophy when he says, "Why, boys, when I was seventeen I walked into the jungle, and when I was twenty-one I walked out . . . And by God I was rich." When sparring with Biff, Ben trips him, threatens him with the point of an umbrella, and then advises, "Never fight fair with a stranger, boy. You'll never get out of the jungle that way." The jungle is clearly the brutal, competitive modern world in which the strong and ruthless like Ben will tri-umph and the weak like Willy will go under.

Here, then, is no image of Willy as destroyer but rather of Willy as victim, coldly fired by the firm he has served for thirty-four years. "Business is business," says the young employer whom Willy has known as a child. Willy agrees that business is business, but he does not really believe it. When he tries to explain why he chose to remain a salesman, he says, " 'Cause what could be more satisfying than to be able to go, at the age of eighty-four, into twenty or thirty different cities, and pick up a phone, and be remembered and loved and helped by so many different people?" Willy's error, as we see him here, is a failure to understand the harshness of the world he has attempted so ineptly to conquer. He has tried to find a world of private affections where there was only a jungle.

—Arthur Ganz, "Arthur Miller: Eden and After," *Realms of the Self: Variations on a Theme in Modern Drama* (New York: New York University Press, 1980), pp. 125–28

C. W. E. Bigsby on the Conclusion of *Death of a Salesman*

[C. W. E. Bigsby (b. 1941), Senior Lecturer in American Literature at the University of East Anglia (Norwich, England), is a prolific scholar on American drama. He has written monographs on Edward Albee (1969), Tom Stoppard (1976), Joe Orton (1982), and David Mamet (1985), as well as such studies as *Modern American Drama 1945–1990* (1992). In this extract, from his three-volume introduction to American drama, Bigsby finds an ambiguity at the end of Miller's play: it is unclear whether Willy's son Biff has genuinely found a new vision of life or will merely lapse back into the values his father held.]

⟨. . .⟩ there is an ambiguity to the play's conclusion. Biff has acquired a crucial insight into himself. Presumably the striving is over, and he can now accept that simple harmony with the natural world which had always foundered on his persistent need for a material success which would appease his father and free him from his guilt. Certainly that is the only real value which has been identified—a lyricism strongly contrasted with the diminished world of urban America. He can return West to the one place where he was really happy. The problem is that on the one hand his flight to the West had originally also been a flight from responsibility, and on the other it is an ahistorical move. Like Huck Finn at the end of Twain's novel, he is lighting out for the territory ahead of the rest. But the rest will inevitably follow, and Miller admitted as much a few years later when, in *The Misfits,* the beautiful mare and its colt are rounded up by trucks and turned into dog food. Biff Loman has become Gay, an ageing cowboy as bewildered by the collapse of his world as Willy Loman had been. And so Biff, who at the end of *Death of a Salesman* has supposedly learned the lesson which Willy could not, seems to be committed to the old mistake of seeking in movement and in space what he should perhaps have sought in relationship. Indeed, when Miller returned to the stage in 1964, after a nine-year silence, it was with a play in which grace is the reward of suffering, and meaning the result of a love constantly renewed in the face of acknowledged imperfection. Like Steinbeck in *The Grapes of Wrath* he ends with a piety whose emotional force is undeniable but whose social utility is more problematic because he can conceive of no mechanism whereby Biff's moment of epiphany can be translated into social action. And that equivocation hangs suspended in the air, inhibiting the sense of completion towards which the play has seemed to move and projecting forward into all our futures a dilemma not so easily resolved by a moment of insight, by a seemingly purposeful action or by an articulate statement of intent. History has moved on and Miller's characters in *Death of a Salesman* seem close kin finally to Scott Fitzgerald's in *The Great Gatsby*. Corrupted by dreams which simultaneously denied them access to the potential redemption of human connectiveness, they had reached out for some substitute for the meaning which continued to elude them. They sought it mostly in an endlessly deferred future, a green light which beckoned them on towards a mythical world of romance and affluence. But at the end of the novel the narrator tries to find it in the past, a rural world where the dream was first born and where the corruption first started. Biff does much the same here, for the world of rural simplicity to which he will now presumably return had provided the context for his grandfather's desertion of Willy. It was also where Uncle Ben began his mythic climb to wealth and power, having abandoned his search for his lost father. The frontier bred the disease. And if it also represents a natural world of pure process then even that is under pressure. Like the land surrounding the

Loman home it will presumably itself one day make way for the city and its cruelties. And so Biff, like Nick Carraway, seems poised for a deeply ambiguous and even ironic journey. So that if Willy, like Gatsby, believed in the green light, 'the orgastic future that year by year recedes before us', a future which 'eluded us then, but that's no matter—tomorrow we will run faster, stretch out our arms further . . . And one fine morning', he and Biff alike are also, perhaps, no more nor less than "boats against the current, borne back ceaselessly into the past" ⟨*The Great Gatsby*⟩.

—C. W. E. Bigsby, "Arthur Miller," *A Critical Introduction to Twentieth-Century American Drama, Volume 2: Tennessee Williams, Arthur Miller, Edward Albee* (Cambridge: Cambridge University Press, 1984), pp. 185–86

GEORGE E. WELLWARTH ON WILLY LOMAN AS A SYNTHETIC MAN

[George E. Wellwarth (b. 1932) is a professor of theatre and comparative literature at the State University of New York at Binghamton and author of *The Theatre of Protest and Paradox* (1964; rev. 1971), *Spanish Underground Drama* (1972), and other works. In this extract, Wellwarth believes that Willy Loman is a "synthetic man" in that his entire view of the world and himself has been shaped by the mechanized society in which he lives.]

A good example of an unintentionally synthetic drama in a "free" society is Arthur Miller's *Death of a Salesman*. Miller's intention was clearly twofold: to write an analytic drama posing the problem of the ordinary worker in a conscienceless, capitalistic society and implicitly condemning the system; and to write a modern tragedy adapting Aristotelian theory to allow for a common man as tragic protagonist. Miller's success in achieving his stated aims has been the subject of considerable debate, principally among those critics who feel that an adherence to Aristotelian guidelines for the writing of tragedy is still important. Miller himself has argued that tragedy consists of "the underlying fear of being displaced, the disaster inherent in being torn away from our chosen image of what and who we are in the world." As a definition of tragedy this is perhaps as valid as any, but it does not apply to Miller's protagonist. Willy Loman is indeed torn away from his image of what and who he is in the world, but that image was never chosen by him. Willy is under the delusion that he has chosen his self-image, but it has in fact been chosen for him, as it has been for the millions who make up the common horde that Miller intends Willy to represent. It is here that the feedback mechanism of the socio-human machine becomes evident. The common man has not chosen his self-image, nor has it been deliberately devised by some powerful individual Machiavellian mind and artfully insinuated to him as his own. The common man's relation to the social machine is a symbiotic one, and the creation of his image of himself is accomplished reciprocally between himself and the multiplication of himself that constitutes the major part of society. It is based simultaneously on the need of the mass to cohere and form the mortar that holds itself together and the individual's need to belong to something other than him-self—in short, to bow down to something greater than himself. Willy Loman and those he represents are the victims of a delusion collectively created by themselves and believed in and worshiped as fervently as any deity ever was. Willy's mind is incapable of independent thought and therefore of self-realization. It is a befuddled mess of slogans derived from the flimflam of advertising jargon and the cant of popularized palliative psychology. And he uses these stock phrases as verbal talismans to ward off reality and self-realization, much as the invocation of imagined creatures in another world was once believed effective in warding off the imagined evil of this one.

Willy Loman is the compleat synthetic man as well as the prototypical common man Miller intends him to be. Willy *believes*. He believes in the myths of the capitalistic society in which he is subsumed. He believes in the myth of log cabin to president, which he transforms into a myth of seedy drudge to big business executive. He believes in the pot of gold at the end of the rainbow, realized in his mind by his brother Ben who walked into the jungle and came out rich. He believes in appearance, in phoniness, in acceptance ("not just liked, but well liked") by those he regards as the gods of the machine. Above all, he believes in advertising slogans: "Chevrolet, Linda, is the greatest car ever built." But somehow his faith does not sustain him ("That goddam Chevrolet, they ought to prohibit the manufacture of that car"), and he has to work harder and harder, bolster his self-delusion more and more to sustain his feeling of integration. At the end he is spewed out by the machine as a useless part and desperately immolates himself in his faith by dying so his son can collect the insurance money and thus pay his entrance fee at the portals of the machine he had left to seek the hard reality of self-realization.

—George E. Wellwarth, *Modern Drama and the Death of God* (Madison: University of Wisconsin Press, 1986), pp. 144–45

NEIL CARSON ON REAL TIME AND REMEMBERED TIME IN *DEATH OF A SALESMAN*

[Neil Carson is a professor of English at the University of Guelph in Guelph, Ontario. He has written *A Companion to Henslowe's Diary* (1988) and *Arthur Miller* (1988), from which the following extract is taken. Here, Carson believes that *Death of a Salesman* constantly operates on two levels—real time and remembered time—and that, as a result, a reading of the play as a mere social criticism is too simplistic.]

It is the very richness of *Death of a Salesman* which is at once its greatest strength and its principal problem. On the one hand, the form permits an intricate interweaving of thematic material in which incidents are thrust into the play with a minimum of exposition and developed only so long as they are thematically relevant. On the other hand, the mixture of verbal and theatrical images defies simple analysis and conveys to many readers and spectators an impression of narrative confusion. This is largely due to the fact that the story proceeds in two dimensions—real time and remembered time. The 'external plot' deals with the last twenty-four hours of Willy's life from his return home late Sunday night to his death Monday evening. Then there is the 'internal plot' which treats the past from Willy's earliest memories of his own father to the fateful summer of Biff's failure in high school. In outline, the play is very similar to an Ibsenite play of ripe circumstance except that the exposition of events from the past is dramatised instead of being simply reported. This similarity makes it possible to discuss the work as a play of social criticism not unlike *All My Sons* in which one might look for the central conflict in the opposed value-systems of the two main characters. According to such a view, *Salesman* is an indictment of the American capitalist system which values machines more highly than men. The central scene takes place in Howard's office where Willy's pleading for his job and invoking his human connection with Howard is cruelly juxtaposed with Howard's indifferent insistence that 'business is business' and with the mechanical imitation of human voices on the wire recorder. The difficulty with this interpretation is that it simplifies the play, ignoring the humane capitalist, Charley, and forgetting altogether that Willy is a very active collaborator in his own downfall.

Another related approach to the play is to see it as a domestic social drama in which the central character is Biff. This interpretation would identify the central conflict as being between Willy's determination to make Biff into a success in capitalistic terms, and his son's search for a more valid life as a man who works with his hands. Here the playwright's earlier examinations of father–son conflicts in *Luck* and *Sons* seem to anticipate the opposition between Willy's phoney doctrine of materialistic success and Biff's perception of a more humane ideal based on the freedom and companionship of the American west. But once again such an interpretation seems a distortion of the play. While it is true that Biff represents the possibility of undeluded integrity, it is not clear precisely what kind of social order he embodies, nor is it at all apparent that we are to prefer Biff's rather unimaginative bumbling to his father's irrepressible hopefulness. Finally, the experience of the play makes it impossible for spectators or readers to respond to Biff as the central character because of the overwhelming presence of Willy.

—Neil Carson, *Arthur Miller* (New York: St. Martin's Press, 1988), pp. 46–48

LEAH HADOMI ON BIFF, HAPPY, AND CHARLEY

[Leah Hadomi is Senior Lecturer of Comparative Literature at Haifa University in Israel. She has written several articles on drama and on the postwar German novel and cinema. In this extract, Hadomi studies Willy's sons, Biff and Happy, and his neighbor Charley, showing how they each reflect a facet of Willy's personality or of other crucial figures in the play.]

Three of the characters among the principal *dramatis personae* of the play, Biff, Happy and Charley, function in the real world as analogous to the ideal types in Willy's consciousness. Though none of them is a complete substantiation of Willy's ego ideals, there is in each character a dominant trait that identifies him with either Willy's father, or Ben, or Dave Singleman, and that determines Willy's relationship to him.

Biff most closely resembles his grandfather in rejecting the constraints imposed by the middle-class routines of holding down a job and making a living, and in his preference for the life of a drifter out West, working as a hired farm-hand in the outdoors. He has a strong touch of the artist and dreamer in his temperament. He is also the most complex character of the three, the most at odds with himself. In this he closely resembles Willy. Like his father, Biff is torn between rural nostalgia and his need for solid achievement, and is tormented by the knowledge of personal failure. "I've always made a point of not wasting my life," he tells Happy, and then confesses to him, "and everytime I come back here I know that all I've done is to waste my life."

Happy corresponds to Ben, if only in a meager and debased way. He shares his uncle's unscrupulousness and amorality, but has little of his singleness of purpose; and what he has of the last he dedicates to cuckolding his superiors at work and to the pursuit of women in general, activities that make up the only field in which he excels, as Linda recognizes when she sums him up as a "philandering bum." He resembles Ben, too, in the shallowness of his filial emotions. The trite praise he bestows on Linda—"What a woman! They broke the mold when they made her"—is on its own vulgar level as perfunctory and unfeeling as Ben's more elegantly phrased endorsement, "Fine specimen of a lady, Mother." However, some of his traits remind us of Willy, such as his bluster and nursing of injured pride, his insecurity about making good, as well as his philandering.

Charley is Dave Singleman brought down to earth. He has none of Singleman's flamboyance that Willy so rapturously remembers from his younger days. Rather, he is successful salesmanship domesticated. Singleman worked out of a hotel room. Charley maintains an office with a secretary and an accountant. He is stolid but honest and decent, and though not loved like Singleman, he is respected. And, by Willy's own startled admission toward the end, he is Willy Loman's only friend. He is also Willy's perfect foil, a man at peace with what he is and his place in the world.

Excepting Charley, the principal characters of *Death of a Salesman* share the same condition of being torn between the conflicting claims of ideality and actuality; and in this capacity the interrelations among them serve to extend and reinforce the rhythmic articulation of the play on a variety of formal levels. Among the consequences of the inner conflicts and contradictions of Willy Loman and his sons is their uncertainty and confusion concerning their own identities, a circumstance of which each shows himself to be aware at some point in the play. So Biff reveals to his mother, "I just can't take hold, Mom. I can't take hold of some kind of a life"; Happy tells Biff, "I don't know what the hell I'm workin' for . . . And still, goddamit, I'm lonely"; and Willy confesses to Ben, "I still feel—kind of temporary about myself."

Willy Loman's attitude to the real characters of the play is determined by their relation to the corresponding ideal types in his mind. None of the real characters is an unalloyed embodiment of these exemplars, who have all been debased to varying degrees in their corporeal counterparts. So, for example, Willy's most complex and ambivalent relationship is with Biff, who is associated most closely with Willy's absolute ego ideal. It is of his older son that Willy had always expected the most, and it is Biff's failure to live up to his expectations that grieves him the most. By comparison his relationship with Happy, of whom he expects much less, is straightforward and indifferent. Willy's relationship with Charley, too, is determined by Charley's proximity to the ideal and his own distance therefrom. Because Charley comes closest of anyone Willy knows to the attainable ideal he has set himself but failed to achieve, he treats him with a mixture of respect and envy. The last prevents Willy from accepting Charley's offer of a job, because doing so would be tantamount to an admission of failure, a reason never stated explicitly by Willy but of which Charley is aware, as we learn during Willy's visit to Charley's office in the second act:

> CHARLEY: What're you, jealous of me?
> WILLY: I can't work for you, that's all, don't ask me why.
> CHARLEY: (*Angered, takes out more bills*) You been jealous of me all your life, you damned fool! Here, pay your insurance.

By taking money from Charley, instead, in the guise of a loan, Willy is able both to retain his self-esteem and to cling to his self-delusions. In a rare moment of candor Willy privately admits to Charley's virtues and superiority to himself ("a man of few words, and they respect him"), but for the most part he seeks to establish his own pre-eminence by belittling and hectoring him in petty ways, reminding Charley of his ignorance and inadequacy in ordinary matters: domestic repairs, diet, clothing, sports, cards, and so on.

—Leah Hadomi, "Fantasy and Reality: Dramatic Rhythm in *Death of a Salesman*," *Modern Drama* 31, No. 2 (June 1988): 161–62

[Kay Stanton is a professor of English at California State University at Fullerton and author of articles on Shakespeare, Christopher Marlowe, and John Milton. In the following extract, Stanton examines the response of the characters to Willy Loman's death, particularly that of his wife, Linda. Stanton concludes that it is the unrelentingly masculine American Dream that killed Willy.]

As the male characters present their competing versions of who Willy was and what he represents, it becomes evident that they understand him less than Linda does. Each identifies himself with Willy, making a male synthesis to contrast and outdo Linda. Biff relates to the camaraderie and construction, the "nice days" such as "Sundays, making the stoop." Forgetting that the stoop was constructed from stolen materials, Biff muses fondly, "there's more of him in that front stoop than in all the sales he ever made." Linda's reply may be meant as a punning sexual tribute: "He was so wonderful with his hands." But then Biff says his famous lines, "He had the wrong dreams. All, all, wrong." Happy responds angrily, but Biff continues, "He never knew who he was," speaking as much about himself as Willy. Charley begins his "Nobody dast blame this man" speech partly to break up a pending fight between the boys. Oddly, in saying what a salesman is, Charley has to specify what he is not, including "He don't put a bolt to a nut"—which Willy actually did, albeit not as a salesman. Charley also is talking partly about himself: he has been the one unaccustomed to using the tools of reconstruction. Furthermore, it is Charley, the unsentimental, non-dreaming realist, who now says, "A salesman is got to dream, boy. It comes with the territory," thus combining his reality with acceptance of Willy's dream. This speech does little to reconcile Biff and Happy, who ignore it and continue their rivalry. Once again, Biff suggests his fraternal dream—that Happy go with him—but Happy says, "I'm not licked that easily" and refers once more to his fraternal dream, "The Loman Brothers!" Happy reaffirms the part of Willy that he identifies with: "the only dream you can have—to come out number-one man." He plans to show Biff and everybody else that Willy Loman did not die in vain.

What Willy did die for if not in vain is not clear in any of the characters' minds, particularly not in Happy's, because not much earlier he had denied that Willy had any "right" to kill himself. Happy's speech is meant to be received by the audience as pathetic, and it is. For one, it defines the only dream possible as coming out "number-one man," women excluded, other men trampled beneath. Biff has now rejected it and turns to his mother. But Linda sends the men on their way, so that she, the only one who truly loved Willy, can be alone with him, and the flute music plays through her speech.

Alone at his grave, Linda asks Willy to forgive her for not being able to cry. Her loyalty and dedication to Willy are such that she wishes to do the expected, appropriate, female supportive behavior even when Willy is no longer there to require it. The two notes sounded alternatively throughout the speech are that she cannot cry and she cannot understand it. Thus part of what she cannot understand is why she cannot cry. On the one hand, Willy's death seems like just another of his absences, when she carries on, managing the bills, etc., as always. She has made the last payment on the house today, and "there'll be nobody home," considering herself, as Willy had, to be nobody. But suddenly a sob rises as she says, "We're free and clear." The idea of freedom releases her to sob more fully: "We're free . . . We're free." What she cannot yet sort out, perhaps, is that she could not cry for Willy because of her unconscious sense of his oppression of her and her sons. She will no longer have to bend under the burden of the masculine ego. Biff is free of the patriarch now, and so is she: free and crying in the emotional intensity that her freedom releases.

Although mystified to seem otherwise, the male American Dream of *Death of a Salesman* is, as the play shows, unbalanced, immature, illogical, lying, thieving, self-contradictory, and self-destructive. Only Willy literally kills himself, but the Dream's celebration of the masculine mythos is inherently self-destructive in its need to obliterate other men or be obliterated, to castrate or be castrated. It prefers to destroy itself rather than to acknowledge the female as equal or to submit to a realistic and balanced feminine value system. This tragedy of the common *man* also wreaks the suffering of the common *woman,* who has trustingly helped the man to maintain and repair the Dream and has helplessly watched him destroy it and render her sacrifices meaningless. One could argue that Linda as common woman possesses more tragic nobility than Willy. Her only flaw was in harnessing all of her talents and energies to support the self-destructive American masculine mythos that requires Woman's subjugation and exploitation. Yet, at the end of the play, Linda lives—and even, for once, gets the last word. Biff, under her unacknowledged influence, now even shows her some tenderness as they leave the stage. But Happy exits last, alone, with the male music of the flute remaining, reminding us of the perpetuation of the Dream.

Thus the audience and readers are left with a choice between Happy and Linda, as Willy had had a choice between Ben and Linda. We can continue to side with the immature masculine mythos in degrading and ignoring Woman while making her the scapegoat for failures in American male-dominated society, or we can free Woman to rise from her oppression by choosing with her the appreciation of love and compassion, the recognition of the values of human dignity, and the worthwhile contributions of men *and* women.

> —Kay Stanton, "Women and the American Dream of *Death of a Salesman," Feminist Rereadings of Modern American Drama,* ed. Jane Schlueter (Rutherford, NJ: Fairleigh Dickinson University Press, 1989), pp. 94–96

DAVID SAVRAN ON THE FEAR OF EFFEMINACY IN *DEATH OF A SALESMAN*

[David Savran (b. 1950) is a professor of English at Brown University and the author of *In Their Own Words: Contemporary American Playwrights* (1988). In this extract from his recent study of Arthur Miller and Tennessee Williams, Savran shows how Miller's play reveals a fear of effeminacy that fuels much of the anxiety found in Willy, Biff, and other characters.]

The fantasy of a community defined by strictly homosocial bonds and yet aggressively heterosexual in its professed orientation puts enormous stress on the already fractured male subject, the one who must exert a control as rigorous over his own desires as over the desires of others. For in addition to demanding the exclusion of effeminate men, this fantasy also requires him to police the feminine within him, those wild and disorderly desires that threaten both the material integrity of the body and the coherence of the social group. In *Salesman,* neither Willy nor Biff is able to coax his masculinist fantasy into reality insofar as both are, in very different ways, tainted by the feminine. Willy's guilty secret, his adulterous liaison with an ungovernable woman whose effusions infect not only his own integrity but Biff's as well, is his ruin and threatens both his own masculine self-sufficiency and the very stability and durability of the patrilineal economy. Since that fatal day in Boston, Biff has lost his way, become a compulsive liar and thief, declining in initiative, feeling "mixed up very bad," the prey of despair and "self-loathing." Unlike his more alluring brother, to whom "sexuality" clings "like a visible color," Biff has a "worn air." Questioned by Happy, he denies that he "still run[s] around a lot" with women and protests mournfully, "I don't know—what I'm supposed to want."

For Biff, the moment of catastrophe (and the play's climactic disclosure) is his witness of the primal scene between his father and the woman "with resistance" who does not happen to be his mother. As replayed in the salesman's memory, Willy hears the knocking at his hotel room door and convinces The Woman to take refuge in the bathroom. When Biff enters, he explains to Willy that he flunked math and will not be able to graduate and go on to be a football star at the University of Virginia, as both had expected. Willy tells Biff that he will talk to his math teacher, Mr. Birnbaum, and, in an effort to get rid of Biff, asks him to go downstairs and inform the clerk that he is checking out. Rather than leaving, however, Biff suddenly decides to tell his father why Mr. Birnbaum "hates" him (although Biff's delay is requisite to the plot, his proffered information is purely gratuitous):

> One day he was late for class so I got up at the blackboard and imitated him. I crossed my eyes and talked with a lithp.

Willy is greatly amused by the story and so Biff continues, in imitation of his lisping teacher:

> The thquare root of thixthy twee is . . . *Willy bursts out laughing; Biff joins him.* And in the middle of it he walked in!

At that juncture Willy laughs again, and "The Woman joins in offstage." When Biff asks if someone's there, she laughs a second time and he naively voices his alarm: "Somebody got in your bathroom!" At this point she enters, lisping like Mr. Birnbaum, "Can I come in?" while Biff just stares "open-mouthed and horrified at The Woman."

This scene explicitly thematizes a symmetry between the two lisping individuals who barge in unexpectedly and sabotage the hopes of Loman father and son: The Woman and Mr. Birnbaum. I believe, however, that this scene has such undeniable power because of another, less explicit, but far more disruptive identification. Just as The Woman and Linda Loman are indissolubly linked (as the uncontained is to the contained) to become the sign of an acute anxiety regarding female discourse and the geography of women's bodies, so are Mr. Birnbaum and Biff linked (as an original is to its imitation) to become the sign of the fear that the feminine always inheres inside the male subject. I make this point not to imply that Biff—or the hapless Mr. Birnbaum, for that matter—is homosexual, but rather to demonstrate the constitutive role that the dread of a feminine male plays in the construction of the authoritative Cold War masculinity for which Miller's protagonists yearn.

—David Savran, *Communists, Cowboys, and Queers: The Politics of Masculinity in the Work of Arthur Miller and Tennessee Williams* (Minneapolis: University of Minnesota Press, 1992), pp. 40–41

Works by
Arthur Miller

Situation Normal. 1944.

Focus. 1945.

All My Sons. 1947.

Death of a Salesman: Certain Private Conversations in Two Acts and a Requiem. 1949.

An Enemy of the People by Henrik Ibsen (adaptor). 1951.

The Crucible. 1953.

A View from the Bridge ⟨with *A Memory of Two Mondays*⟩: *Two One-Act Plays.* 1955.

Collected Plays. 1957–81. 2 vols.

The Misfits. 1961.

Jane's Blanket. 1963.

After the Fall. 1964.

Incident at Vichy. 1965.

I Don't Need You Any More: Stories. 1967, 1987 (as *The Misfits and Other Stories*).

The Price. 1968.

In Russia (with Inge Morath). 1969.

The Portable Arthur Miller. Ed. Harold Clurman. 1971.

The Creation of the World and Other Business. 1973.

In the Country (with Inge Morath). 1977.

Theatre Essays. Ed. Robert A. Martin. 1978.

Chinese Encounters (with Inge Morath). 1979.

Eight Plays. 1981.

Playing for Time: A Screenplay. 1981.

The American Clock. 1982.

Elegy for a Lady. 1982.

Some Kind of Love Story. 1983.

Salesman in Beijing. 1984.

The Archbishop's Ceiling. 1984.

Two-Way Mirror: A Double-Bill of Elegy for a Lady and Some Kind of Love Story. 1984.

Playing for Time: A Full-Length Stage Play. 1985.

Danger: Memory! A Double-Bill of I Can't Remember Anything and Clara. 1986.

Timebends: A Life. 1987.

Conversations with Arthur Miller. Ed. Matthew C. Roudane. 1987.

Plays: One. 1988.

The Archbishop's Ceiling; The American Clock. 1988.

Plays: Two. 1988.

The Golden Years and The Man Who Had All the Luck. 1989.

Early Plays. 1989.

On Censorship and Laughter. 1990.

Plays: Three. 1990.

Everybody Wins: A Screenplay. 1990.

The Last Yankee. 1991.

The Ride Down Mount Morgan. 1991.

Homely Girl: A Life (with Louis Bourgeois). 1992. 2 vols.

Broken Glass. 1994.

The Last Yankee; with a New Essay, About Theatre Language; and Broken Glass. 1994.

Plays: Four. 1994.

Works about Arthur Miller and *Death of a Salesman*

Aarnes, William. "Tragic Form and the Possibility of Meaning in *Death of a Salesman.*" *Furman Studies* 29 (1983): 57–80.

Adam, Julie. *Versions of Heroism in Modern American Drama: Redefinitions by Miller, Williams, O'Neill, and Anderson.* New York: St. Martin's Press, 1991.

August, Eugene R. "*Death of a Salesman:* A Men's Studies Approach." *Western Ohio Journal* 7 (1986): 53–71.

Babcock, Granger. "'What's the Secret?' Willy Loman as Desiring Machine." *American Drama* 2 (1992): 59–83.

Bates, Barclay W. "The Lost Past in *Death of a Salesman.*" *Modern Drama* 11 (1968–69): 164–72.

Bhatia, Santosh K. *Arthur Miller: Social Drama as Tragedy.* New Delhi: Arnold-Heinemann, 1985.

Bigsby, C. W. E. *Confrontation and Commitment: A Study of Contemporary American Drama.* Columbia: University of Missouri Press, 1967.

———, ed. *File on Miller.* London: Methuen, 1988.

Bloom, Harold, ed. *Arthur Miller.* New York: Chelsea House, 1987.

———, ed. *Arthur Miller's* Death of a Salesman. New York: Chelsea House, 1988.

———, ed. *Willy Loman.* New York: Chelsea House, 1990.

Blumberg, Paul. "Sociology and Social Literature: Work Alienation in the Plays of Arthur Miller." *American Quarterly* 21 (1969): 291–310.

Brucher, Richard T. "Willy Loman and the Soul of a New Machine: Technology and the Common Man." *Journal of American Studies* 17 (1983): 325–36.

Brustein, Robert. "Arthur Miller's Mea Culpa." *New Republic,* 8 February 1964, pp. 26–30.

Centola, Steven R. "Family Values in *Death of a Salesman.*" *CLA Journal* 37 (1993–94): 29–41.

Choudhuri, A. D. "*Death of a Salesman:* A Salesman's Illusion." In Choudhuri's *The Face of Illusion in American Drama.* Atlantic Highlands, NJ: Humanities Press, 1979, pp. 94–111.

Corrigan, Robert W., ed. *Arthur Miller: A Collection of Critical Essays.* Englewood Cliffs, NJ: Prentice-Hall, 1969.

"*Death of a Salesman:* A Symposium." *Tulane Drama Review* 2, No. 3 (May 1958): 63–69.

Driver, Tom F. "Strength and Weakness in Arthur Miller." *Tulane Drama Review* 4, No. 4 (May 1960): 45–52.

Dukore, Bernard F. Death of a Salesman *and* The Crucible. Atlantic Highlands, NJ: Humanities Press, 1989.

Eisinger, Chester. "Focus on Arthur Miller's *Death of a Salesman:* The Wrong Dreams." In *American Dreams, American Nightmares,* ed. David Madden. Carbondale: Southern Illinois University Press, 1970, pp. 165–74.

Evans, Richard I. *Psychology and Arthur Miller.* New York: Dutton, 1969.

Ferguson, Alfred R. "The Tragedy of the American Dream in *Death of a Salesman.*" *Thought* 53 (1978): 81–98.

Ganz, Arthur. "The Silence of Arthur Miller." *Drama Survey* 3 (1963): 224–37.

Greenfield, Thomas Allen. *Work and the Work Ethic in American Drama 1920–1970.* Columbia: University of Missouri Press, 1982.

Gross, Barry Edward. "Peddler and Pioneer in *Death of a Salesman.*" *Modern Drama* 7 (1964–65): 405–10.

Hagopian, John V. "Arthur Miller: The Salesman's Two Cases." *Modern Drama* 6 (1963–64): 117–25.

Harder, Harry. "*Death of a Salesman:* An American Classic." In *Censored Books: Critical Viewpoints,* ed. Nicholas J. Karolides, Lee Burress, and John M. Kean. Metuchen, NJ: Scarecrow Press, 1993, pp. 209–19.

Harshbarger, Karl. *The Burning Jungle: An Analysis of Arthur Miller's* Death of a Salesman. Washington, DC: University Press of America, 1980.

Hayman, Ronald. *Arthur Miller.* London: William Heinemann, 1970.

Heilman, Robert B. *The Iceman, the Arsonist and the Troubled Agent: Tragedy and Melodrama on the Modern Stage.* Seattle: University of Washington Press, 1973.

Hurrell, John D., ed. *Two Modern American Tragedies: Reviews and Criticism of* Death of a Salesman *and* A Streetcar Named Desire. New York: Scribner's, 1961.

Hynes, Joseph A. "Attention Must Be Paid . . ." *College English* 23 (1961–62): 574–78.

Jacobson, Irving. "Family Dreams in *Death of a Salesman.*" *American Literature* 47 (1975): 247–58.

Koon, Helen Wickham, ed. Death of a Salesman: *A Collection of Critical Essays.* Englewood Cliffs, NJ: Prentice-Hall, 1983.

Lawrence, Stephen A. "The Right Dream in Miller's *Death of a Salesman.*" *College English* 25 (1963–64): 547–49.

Lewis, Allan. *"Death of a Salesman."* In Lewis's *The Contemporary Theatre: The Significant Playwrights of Our Time.* New York: Crown, 1962, pp. 295–303.

Mander, John. "Arthur Miller's *Death of a Salesman.*" In Mander's *The Writer and Commitment.* London: Secker & Warburg, 1961, pp. 138–52.

Martin, Robert A., ed. *Arthur Miller: New Perspectives.* Englewood Cliffs, NJ: Prentice-Hall, 1982.

Martine, James J., ed. *Critical Essays on Arthur Miller.* Boston: G. K. Hall, 1979.

Meserve, Walter J., ed. *The Merrill Studies in* Death of a Salesman. Columbus, OH: Merrill, 1972.

Moss, Leonard. *Arthur Miller.* New York: Twayne, 1967 (rev. ed. 1980).

Mottram, Eric. "Arthur Miller: The Development of a Political Dramatist in America." In *American Theatre* (Stratford-upon-Avon Studies 10), ed. John Russell Brown and Bernard Harris. London: Edward Arnold, 1967, pp. 127–62.

Murray, Edward. *Arthur Miller, Dramatist.* New York: Ungar, 1967.

Nelson, Benjamin. *Arthur Miller: Portrait of a Playwright.* London: Peter Owen, 1970.

Panikkar, N. Bhaskara. *Individual Morality and Social Happiness in Arthur Miller.* Atlantic Highlands, NJ: Humanities Press, 1982.

Prudhoe, John. "Arthur Miller and the Tradition of Tragedy." *English Studies* 43 (1962): 430–39.

Scanlan, Tom. *Family, Drama, and American Dreams.* Westport, CT: Greenwood Press, 1978.

Schlueter, June, and James K. Flanagan. *Arthur Miller.* New York: Ungar, 1987.

Schroeder, Patricia R. *The Presence of the Past in Modern American Drama.* Rutherford, NJ: Fairleigh Dickinson University Press, 1989.

Shelton, Frank W. "Sports and the Competitive Ethic: *Death of a Salesman* and *That Championship Season.*" *Ball State University Forum* 20, No. 2 (1978): 17–21.

Spindler, Michael. *American Literature and Social Change: William Dean Howells to Arthur Miller.* Bloomington: Indiana University Press, 1983.

Trowbridge, Clinton W. "Arthur Miller: Between Pathos and Tragedy." *Modern Drama* 10 (1967): 221–32.

Vogel, Dan. *The Three Masks of American Tragedy.* Baton Rouge: Louisiana State University Press, 1974.

Welland, Dennis. *Arthur Miller: A Study of His Plays.* London: Methuen, 1979 (3rd rev. ed. 1985 [as *Miller, the Playwright*]).

Index of
Themes and Ideas